MY STORY

FOR GOD'S GLORY

PART TWO

(1967-1987)

MY STORY

FOR GOD'S GLORY
PART TWO
(1967-1987)

Continuing My Lifetime Journey with Jesus
in Far-away Papua New Guinea

By Helen M. Glick

All names and places mentioned in this book
are the actual names of persons and
places as told in the story.

ISBN 978-1-934447-47-5

-Author-
Helen M. Glick
1838 Tremont Ave. SE
Massillon, OH 44646
(330) 830-1452
helenglick@att.net

Published by
Whispering Pines Publishing
11013 Country Pines Road
Shoals, IN 47581

www.countrypinesprinting.com

DEDICATION

This book is lovingly dedicated to all my fellow-missionaries who were a part of our Evangelical Bible Mission Family during the years we lived and worked there. Some of those missionaries are no longer with us, but their memory fondly lingers in my heart, and I am thankful for the influence they have had in my life. I have not pictured these missionary friends in this book, nor have I even mentioned all their names, yet I deeply love and respect each one of them as God's choice of co-laborers with us in doing His work and ministry in Papua New Guinea.

Likewise, I also dedicate this book to all my many students that filled the classrooms where I taught, both in Peniel Christian High School in Ohio, and at every Mission Station where we lived in Papua New Guinea—whether those classes were in schools, in churches, or in our home. All these children and young people were very precious to me, as I endeavored to teach them about the Lord Jesus Christ who loved them and provided eternal Salvation for them—in addition to all the other subjects that were my lot to teach.

And finally, I dedicate this book to all the Pastors, the Teachers, and the faithful Christians of Papua New Guinea who have been carrying the torch of the Gospel of Jesus Christ to their own people—from the time of their conversion even unto this present day—or to the time of their home-going to be with the Lord.

May this book be a blessing and encouragement to all of you.

**GOD BLESS YOU—ONE AND ALL
I LOVE YOU!**

ACKNOWLEDGMENTS

It is indeed with heartfelt appreciation that I express my thanks to all those who have assisted me in different ways to complete my work on this book.

First, I am so grateful for the offer of a long-time friend to proofread and edit my manuscript, and to that person (who wishes to remain anonymous), I want to I say a hearty "thank you"! Also, in the process of preparing my pages for a hard copy to work on, I have developed a deep appreciation and friendship with those who have done lots of copy-work for me at the nearby UPS Store. To each of you I also want to say a big "thank-you" as well.

Last, but not least, I want to again express my loving thanks to my husband, who has assisted me in many ways in the home in order to free up time for me to work at my computer, as well as at the dining-room table. He has also been very patient with my wide spread of papers, cutting-board and photos on the table while working at choosing, cutting, and arranging the photos to be included. I am deeply grateful for that support and encouragement.

Thank you so much!
Helen

TABLE of CONTENTS

<><><><><><><><><>

PHOTO PAGES:
17 / 18 / 29 / 41 / 42 / 51 / 59 / 60 / 66 / 74 / 78 / 83 / 85 / 92 /
93 / 96 / 103 / 104 / 113 / 117 / 118 / 129 / 130 / 141 / 146 /
149 / 150 / 156 / 157 / 168-171 / 173-182

PREFACE

For the reader who did not read *Part One* of **My Story,** it will be helpful to read this brief overview of the story that began in 1934 and is continued here in *Part Two.*

Part One ended in 1967 after my husband and I returned from our first overseas missionary ministry in the Bahamian Islands. In *Part Two,* our journey continues on with two more years of "on-the-job" training at home in USA, further preparing us for the next *long-term* overseas assignment given us by the Lord. That assignment took Daniel and me to far distant parts of the world where we never dreamed of going, and into a primitive culture filled with numerous challenges, exciting adventures, and a whole world of new relationships that will never be forgotten. This assignment lasted more than 18 years, bringing *Part Two* to a close at the end of 1987. The last part of the whole tale will continue our journey through the following years—up to this present year of 2011.

And by the way, (in case you didn't read *Part One)*, the assignment awaiting us when we got home from the Bahamas was for me to teach in the *high school department* of the *Peniel Christian Day School*, (after 10 weeks of summer classes at Malone College.) During those same summer months while I studied at the college, Daniel would be busy building a parsonage for the church. The high school department of the school was to be located in the basement of that house, so I would have my classes there.

I am now eager to share with you more about *God's goodness, mercy,* and *marvelous leadership* in our lives. *Truly HE is a faithful, loving, and dependable GOD*, and there is *NONE other than HE who can make anyone's life truly worth-while for time and eternity.*

The Author

The words of the song on the following page are included here as a constant reminder of God's calling in my life. It was through this song that my heart was moved to fully dedicate my life to *be* *what* ***God*** *wants me to be,* ***go*** *where* ***He*** *wants me to go,* and *say* *what* ***He*** *wants me to say* throughout my entire life. In addition, the Scripture in ***Proverbs 3:5, 6*** provided the stabilizing power that kept my commitment firm, because I was trusting alone in ***Jesus, my Lord and Savior.*** This commitment is the secret of my joy and happiness throughout all the changing circumstances of my life as it progressed over the years. You will read in the pages of this book how many times this commitment has been tested, and how God's grace and wisdom came through to strengthen and guide me again and again for each and every task He laid out before me. To ***Him*** I give all the glory and praise for every victory, and for the wonderful privilege of serving Him—alongside of my husband—whom He gave to be my faithful companion and co-laborer in His work. *PRAISE THE LORD!*

I'll Go Where You Want Me To Go

-1-

It may not be on the mountain height,
Or over the stormy sea,
It may not be at the battle front
My Lord will have need of me;
But if by a still small voice He calls
To paths that I do not know,
I'll answer, dear Lord, with my hand in Thine,
I'll go where you want me to go.

-2-

Perhaps today there are loving words
Which Jesus would have me speak
There may be now in the paths of sin
Some wanderer whom I should seek:
O Savior, if Thou wilt be my guide,
Though dark and rugged the way,
My voice shall echo the message sweet,
I'll say what you want me to say.

-3-

There's surely somewhere a lowly place
In earth's harvest field so wide,
Where I may labor thro' life's short day
For Jesus, the crucified;
So trusting my all to thy tender care,
And knowing Thou lovest me,
I'll do thy will with a heart sincere,
I'll be what you want me to be.

- CHORUS -

I'll go where you want me to go, dear LORD,
Over mountain or plain or sea,
I'll say what you want me to say, dear LORD,
I'll be what you want me to be.

Chapter 1

A TIME for FURTHER TRAINING

Being back home once again with family and friends at church and living in the same community with them was very exciting for us, for now life would be *very different* for us again. It was not long before we got settled into a rented upstairs apartment in Navarre, OH, which would be our home for the next four months. From there I would go to Malone College in Canton, OH, for the summer courses I would be taking at the college, and Daniel would drive to the church property, which was the construction site for the new parsonage.

I cannot recall many details of those days, but I do remember how happy I was to at last begin *what I thought would be* my college education! Since *English* was one of the main subjects that I would be teaching in the high-school department of the Peniel Holiness Christian Day School in the fall, that was the main subject I chose to include in both of the 5-week sessions of the summer-school schedule at the college. Besides that, I also studied *Biology* during the first 5-weeks, and concluded with *Art Appreciation* in the second session. In that way, I was able to complete *the entire first year of college English* during those 10 weeks, and have a semester of *Biology* completed as well. The *Art Appreciation* was a less intensive course that would eventually help me toward the final goal of a completed four-year college education—so I thought.

However, *that dream* was never fulfilled, for God had other plans for me in the future, as you will learn as you continue reading. *God's plans are always best, and the most fulfilling course of action to reach life's eternal goal!* It is with joy that I look back on the events that followed, and I praise God for the way He was leading Daniel and me on our journey through life at that time—step by step. As the summer months sped by, the parsonage was finally completed and ready for the pastor and his family to move in. We also made a move from the apartment in Navarre to the farm house across the highway from the school where I would be teaching. Esther Hershey, one of the Primary teachers of the school, was already living in the upstairs of that house, so Daniel and I would be living on the first floor only. It was a very handy place for both Esther and I to live since we could easily walk to and from our work at the school each day.

The high school department of the school was to be located in the basement of the new parsonage, so there is where I would have my classes, along with Millard and Naomi Downing (our Pastor and wife), and another young teacher, Jo Eleanor Jones. I don't recall what all their subjects were, but for me it was *English Grammar*, *General Business*, and *Home Economics*. I do recall, however, that one subject Jo Eleanor taught was *Spanish Grammar*, and Brother Downing taught the *Bible subjects* while Sister Downing taught *Typing*. Besides that, I don't remember who taught what. Nevertheless, I also recall that I enjoyed the anticipation and challenge of teaching there so very much; and having refreshed my knowledge of *English Grammar* during the summer at Malone College, I felt ready to tackle the job of teaching *that* subject with pleasure! (*English Literature* was not a part of the required curriculum at that particular time, and I was glad, for I was *not qualified* to tackle that phase of the English course.)

Our school was small, so teachers and students learned to know each other quite well—so well, in fact, that some of my students pulled a prank on me one day! Just listen to what they did!

A MEMORABLE PRANK
ON AN UNSUSPECTING TEACHER

It was my habit, when coming into my afternoon class each day—when the waste can was already piled high with paper, that I would step my foot into the can and press down the paper to allow room for more paper as the day wore on. And so, on this particular day, I did as I always did. But, *WOW! Did I ever get a big surprise!* The can *appeared* to be full of paper as usual, but it was *not really* full of *paper!* Instead, there was paper *only on top of water!* Some prankster had put water there to make a dunce of me! But it was done all in fun, and as you can guess, all the mischievous boys in the classroom could not contain their laughter as I stood there stunned, with a very wet shoe and stocking! I joined in laughing with them, but I did not quite know what to do with my wet foot, shoe, and stocking for the rest of the day.

That is when Brother Downing—the *Principal*, who was in the next room with his class—upon hearing the commotion and laughter in my classroom, came into our room to see what was going on. When he learned what had happened, he ordered the students to settle down to their lessons, yet he himself could hardly keep a straight face until he got out of the room! It was so funny! Then, with concern for my situation, he sent word upstairs to his wife to send down a pair of his heavy woolen socks for me to wear instead of my wet shoe and stocking. He was concerned that being in the colder season of the year, I might catch cold from being on the new concrete floor with wet footwear. For me, however, that idea was the worst part of the whole deal! It was quite humiliating for me to *even think of wearing the Principal's black sock on my foot the rest of the day*. Nevertheless, not wanting to be rude and refuse to accept this show of concern, that is just what I did! I cannot recall how much we actually got done in class from then on that day, but that mischievous prank is one that everyone calls to remembrance when we get together for reunions from time to time. We still have a big laugh about it!

Some time later I learned that it *was my own nephew* who was the one responsible for thinking of the prank—but of course, the other boys in the class were just as delighted to co-operate in the process of making it happen!

AN INTERESTING SUMMER'S ACTIVITIES

With my first year of teaching now over, some new and exciting activities were lined up for Daniel and me for the summer. At the close of the school year, when I learned that Jo Eleanor Jones would not be returning for the next school year, I heard some of her students expressing a desire to learn more Spanish, and to be able to *speak* it. I then asked Brother Downing if he thought there would be some course I could take to learn to *speak* Spanish, so that I could then share what I learned with these students. He did not offer to provide sponsorship for such a course, but he did affirm that if I wanted to do that it would be fine with him. So I went on a search and came across the *BERLITZ SCHOOL of LANGUAGES* which was especially designed for businessmen traveling to foreign countries.

BERLITZ LANGUAGE SCHOOL courses consisted of two, one-and-a-half-hour lessons a day, five days a week, for ten weeks. A native speaker of the language to be learned would be the private instructor, and no English would be spoken—only the language being learned. By the end of the ten weeks, the goal was for the student to be able to travel to that particular country and be able to communicate sufficiently well enough to conduct business there. It sounded terrific for what I wanted to do as well, so we decided to invest in the challenge!

In the meantime, Daniel had also been asked to do some renovation work on some of the buildings at *GOD'S BIBLE SCHOOL* in Cincinnati, OH, during the summer. Since *BERLITZ LANGUAGE SCHOOL* was also located in Cincinnati, things worked out that while Daniel was doing work on the *Girls' Dormitory* and on the *Music Hall* at GBS, I took my course in Spanish! We lived in a dormitory room at the Bible School and had all our meals with the students that were on the campus during the summer. It was a great experience for us, and we loved the interaction with those students! It also gave us an opportunity to accompany the students in their summer city mission activities. We loved those experiences, too! And for me, studying and practicing Spanish most of the day was so much fun! Even Daniel was learning some words and sentences along with me!

The summer finally came to an end, and soon we were back in our home near the school, and a new school year had begun. And—believe-it-or-not—*I actually had a class of students to whom I was doing my best to teach conversational Spanish!* Yes, I was doing my best, but I soon learned that *my best* was not good enough to do the job adequately. Rather, it was a continued learning time for me as well as for my students. And it was the thrill of practicing and learning together with my students that made the time and effort worthwhile for them and for me. (And would you believe it—no less than two out of the five Spanish students that graduated at the end of that school year later became missionaries working in Mexico for many years! Today they and their grown families are able to speak Spanish fluently—*but not to my credit!* They have completely surpassed their fledgling Spanish teacher of their high school days!)

The staff and students of the High School Department
of Peniel Holiness Christian Day School

At my desk with Robert Miller

Waiting to begin my day with my students

Students at work in their classroom

The house where Daniel and I and Esther Hershey lived while I was teaching at Peniel

Chapter 2

YEAR TWO at PENIEL

As the new school year began with its new challenges, I was not only teaching English, but also conversational Spanish and bookkeeping. Using my bookkeeping textbook from high school, it was an enjoyable experience to pass on to two classes of students what I had learned from that high school textbook. A new group of ten freshman girls were students in one of those classes. They were *lots of fun* to teach! I loved all my students very much, and enjoyed the privilege of teaching them things I had learned in life thus far along the way.

Then, in the meantime, we were invited to visit some missionary friends in Mexico, so that trip was planned for December. It was there that our friends, Jimmy and Mary Waud, introduced us to our first foreign missionary experience where English was not the spoken language. I was really happy, because now, by visiting a Spanish-speaking country, I could at last put to practice some of the Spanish I had learned. On one occasion when I did so, I made an awful blunder that is too embarrassing to repeat here. It was spoken in answer to a question addressed to me by a group of women. When the missionary laughingly asked me if I knew what I had said—because the ladies were all laughing at my response—I told her I only knew *what I meant to say!* Apparently what I meant to say hadn't been said correctly, making my response *embarrassingly* laughable! When I realized my mistake, I laughed with them; but I also knew it would take a lot more study and continual practice to use the right words and say things correctly!

Jimmy and Mary's ministry was near the Texas border, where we helped with special meetings, including lots of children. I had taken my accordion, and when we went home, I left it behind for Mary because hers was worn out. I cannot include here all the details of that wonderful visit, but among other interesting things we did, we also had the privilege of traveling nearly to the center of the country. In that way we got a glimpse of what the country was like away from the border, and how the people lived there as well. We traveled as far as we could in a van, distributing gospel tracts along the way wherever we could. At one town we left our van, going the rest of the way on horseback (where the van couldn't go) to a smaller village area. Riding horseback was a new and *jolting* experience for both of us! (Actually, my steed was a donkey, not a horse!)

ANOTHER KIND of LESSON to be LEARNED

By now, after 15 years of marriage, in spite of the fact that we still had no children, Daniel and I were completely happy and contented in our life of serving the Lord in the different ways the Lord opened up to us. What a blessing it was to have each other, enjoying each other's companionship, doing things together, etc. But would it *always* be that way? What happened next was another new lesson for both of us!

It was during this second year of teaching at the Peniel School, (1968/69), when *a missionary from Bolivia, South America,* came to visit and speak to the student body in chapel-time one day. Daniel came to the school that day to hear his presentation as well. It was really interesting and challenging—especially to Daniel and me. We still had a very deep interest in missions, even though we were no longer away from home on a foreign mission field. In truth, however, what we did not *realize was that we were actually already active as missionaries for God's Kingdom right where we were!* At that time, Daniel had no steady employment, but he worked with his brothers on construction jobs when available. Thus, when the visiting missionary stated that help was urgently needed to complete various carpenter jobs on the mission compound in Bolivia, Daniel's heart was deeply touched with a desire to go there and help them. I, too, felt the same urge—that Daniel should go there to help with this need. Of course, I had a great desire to go with him, but being already busily engaged with my teaching, I knew that I was right where the Lord wanted me for the time being. And because of that, I was willing to let Daniel go while I stayed at home to fill my place in the school.

Decisions like that are not made quickly, but in due time, after earnestly seeking to know God's will about it, that is what we decided to do. And so it was—from early in February until mid-April of 1969—Daniel and I were both busy in the work of the Lord while many hundreds of miles apart. I was teaching school at Peniel, and Daniel was in *Riberalta, Bolivia, in South America*, using his skills at carpentry!

During this trip to Bolivia, Daniel had many interesting experiences he likes to share with others, so I pause here to fill you in on a few of them, even though I was not there with him to experience them first hand.

DANIEL'S BOLIVIA EXPERIENCES

Max Green, the missionary with whom he was traveling to Bolivia, was well able to speak Spanish, but not Daniel. The plane that was taking them southward to their destination was full of Spanish-speaking people, but no one seemed to know English except Max and Daniel.

The first frightening thing that happened on their journey was at *Bogotá, Columbia.* When the plane landed there, two of the tires on the plane blew out! During the landing process, the pilot had a hard time keeping the plane balanced as it rocked back and forth. Hot, smoky rubber from the tires went flying past the window on the other side of the plane from where Daniel was seated! The passengers were detained on the plane, waiting for the fire-truck and ambulance to arrive on the scene. When they were finally able to get off the plane, Daniel got out his camera to take some photos, and in so doing, he got separated from Max. Then, seeing the bus full of people who were being taken to the terminal (about a mile from the plane) Daniel ran quickly and got on it. Though he did not see him, he figured that Max was already on the bus. At the terminal, however, he looked for Max, only to discover he had not been on the bus after all! Because Daniel could speak no Spanish, he could not find anyone to help him know what to do, so he finally decided to walk back to the plane, thinking Max must surely be looking for him! However, on the way he was met by the same bus coming again toward the terminal with another load of passengers. Max was on the bus this time, so the bus stopped and picked up Daniel. At last he and Max were together again! That was quite a scare for him, to say the least!

Before arriving in Bolivia, another incident occurred as his flight was leaving Lima, Peru. From his seat, Daniel noticed a fuel tank cap attached to a small chain laying on the wing of the plane. As the plane taxied down the runway, the cap spun on the chain like it was ready to fly off! Daniel told Max what he was seeing, but Max thought it must be a spare cap, so he wasn't much concerned about it. Daniel, however, was not satisfied with that, so he kept watching closely what would happen next. Then, when the engine revved up for take off, and the brake was released, the fuel came gushing out of the plane as it sped down the runway. By this time, others in the plane were noticing what was going on as well, and as anxiety was mounting, Daniel quickly pulled the cord to call the stewardess. The stewardess quickly got word to the pilot, and just before lift-off, the power of the engine suddenly cut back and the plane was turned around and taken back to where it had departed. There a ladder was quickly put up to the wing, and search was made for the fuel cap. Of course, they did not find it! Then after another cap was put on, the plane was soon on its way again. *Who knows what disaster could have taken place if the Lord had not caused Daniel and others to see what was happening. How worthy of praise is our great God and Savior for His protection!*

Daniel would have many other interesting stories of his time in Bolivia, but I only mention one more here. That is because I almost lost him while he was there! I had been expecting him home at a given time, but just the day before his scheduled departure, he got very sick! He began experiencing severe diarrhea and vomiting at the same time, and was diagnosed to have two strands of amoebic dysentery! Because he had become deathly sick and was extremely weak, word was sent to me that he would have to remain there another ten days to get the proper treatment of medication at the near-by hospital. After that extra time of patiently waiting, I was so thankful when I knew he was finally coming home from his ten weeks of absence. When he arrived at the airport, he looked so pale and thin that I could hardly recognize him—but oh, how good it was to have him home with me once again! (That was the longest separation we have ever had—before or since then!) How good the Lord was to both of us during that time, for He gave us both the needed grace and strength to occupy patiently until the separation was over! And through it, He allowed Daniel to leave a positive testimony for Jesus in the land of Bolivia!

(In retrospect, I often wish I could have shared all those Bolivia experiences with Daniel, yet at that time I was thankful that we were both doing the task the Lord had given us to do, and His blessing was upon us both just where we were. We learned a lot through that experience!)

After Daniel's time in Bolivia, I continued teaching in the school to the end of the school year. It had been another wonderful year of helping to prepare my students for what God had in store for them in the future. At that time I never dreamed that my being at Peniel those two years was giving me an opportunity to share in the harvest of what *He had planned* for the lives of my students in the years ahead. Of the two classes that graduated those two years—1968 and 1969, here is a list of how God has used these eight students for His glory in different ways, in different lands, and in different cultures:

~~~~~~~~~~~~~~~~~~~~~~

>*Henry Miller* married a minister's daughter and became a preacher, pastor, and traveling evangelist here in USA. He and his family are also excellent musicians and evangelistic singers as well.

>*Lane Glick* and *Robert Miller*, together with their spouses and families, were called of God to work as missionaries in Papua New Guinea.

>*Cathy Helsel* and *David Weaver* were also called of the Lord, together with their spouses and families, to work as missionaries caring for orphans in Mexico.

>*Clara Miller* worked as a single missionary nurse in Haiti; later she also married, with two of her sons becoming medical doctors and her daughter a nurse.

>*Mae Miller* and her brother *Steven* did not become missionaries working in foreign lands, but they also lived exemplary lives for Jesus in their churches and families, doing business and ministry activities that honored God here in the homeland.

~~~~~~~~~~~~~~~~~~~~~~

I have included this follow-up information about these students because it demonstrates the faithfulness of our Lord as He works and moves in the lives of youth who are taught the way of Salvation and have received Him as their Lord and Savior, understanding the importance of loving God and serving Him with their whole life. *TO GOD BE ALL THE GLORY FOR ALL HE*

DOES! Today these same students are faithfully serving the Lord in various ways. Even though, to my knowledge, none of them are any longer on a foreign mission field, their children and their families also are now living exemplary lives for Christ Jesus, helping to support missionaries and their ministries in various locations in the world.

AN OPEN DOOR THAT DID NOT CLOSE

As this 2nd school year was coming to a close, even others around us began to sense that our hearts and minds were ready to be launching out on a new missionary venture. We had no knowledge or idea, however, of what or where that would be, but we just felt the urge in our spirit that something was about to change again. Then all at once doors began to open to us, with invitations for us to go to Mexico, to Bolivia, back to the Bahamas, or to work with the Navajo Brethren-in-Christ Mission in New Mexico. We felt no clear leadership of the Holy Spirit as to which—*if any* of these places—it would be. Nevertheless, as we prayed and waited on the Lord, one by one these same doors began to close for one reason or another. That is—all but Mexico. Really, I personally had a strong desire to go to a Spanish-speaking country (where I could learn more Spanish), and it seemed like Mexico might be the right place for us. I was rather excited about that, yet neither of us had personal peace about it. So, together we kept praying and waiting for a confirmation from the Lord before committing ourselves to even applying for a place in this ministry. Then something quite unusual happened one evening while we were eating supper at our house.

Our phone rang, and it was a long-distance phone call—which in those days was something very unusual for us. The phone call came from *GOD'S BIBLE SCHOOL*—from the school's *President* himself! While Daniel was working there at the school during the previous summer, *President Samuel Deets* had become friends with us, and he was well aware that we were keenly interested in foreign missionary work. Having recently learned that we were looking forward to serving again somewhere, he called to ask us a question that might help us and give us guidance. It was this:

"Since you are interested in going to a mission field again, have you considered New Guinea? They are quite urgently in need of workers just now."

"No," we told him, *"We don't know much about New Guinea, and we have not heard anything about the need there—but we will pray about it."*

Actually, we had *once* heard *Gerald Bustin*, a young single missionary from New Guinea, speak at a missionary service at GBS, but being unfamiliar with the country, and not even knowing where New Guinea was located, what we heard at that time did not really register well in our minds. Now, however, with this invitation to work there being presented to us, our attention was stirred up to learn more about the country. We would also definitely make this a special matter of prayer while seeking to find out more about New Guinea and to know God's will and plan for us.

With this new proposal still ringing in our ears and on our minds as we were finishing our meal, even before our meal was finished, the phone rang again! Would you believe it? Once again it was a *long-distance* call from *GOD'S BIBLE SCHOOL!* This time, however, it was the *Director of the Missions Department, Delmar Kauffman,* who had called. He did not know that President Deets had called us, nor had he communicated with him concerning the reason for his call! Yet, what Bro. Kauffman had to say was *almost identical* to what President Deets had said to us a few minutes before! This, we felt, was not just a coincidence; instead, we sensed that *the LORD* was definitely saying something to us! Then Bro. Kauffman suggested that we talk personally with *Earl Adams*, the *Chairman* of *Evangelical Bible Mission.* He was visiting there at the Bible School at that time. He also assured us that truly help was *urgently* and *promptly* needed for their ministry in New Guinea. We then told Bro. Kauffman what we had told President Deets, that *we would make this invitation to work in New Guinea a special matter of prayer, and then we would obey what the Lord was telling us to do.* And of course—that is just what we did! In our prayers, we asked the Lord to *close this door* to us (as He had done with other open doors) if it was *NOT His will* for us to accept this challenge.

After that, as the school year was coming to a close, we sensed deeply that the door to working in New Guinea was *still wide open*, and because *we were ready and willing,* there was nothing to stop us from giving a positive answer. From then on, it was not long until we filled out applications, giving names for letters of recommendation for us to work with the *Evangelical Bible Mission*—the Mission Board that was recruiting missionaries for New Guinea.

At last my *second year* of teaching at Peniel was completed, and so was *my time* for teaching there. Our vision was now focused on a different goal. Therefore, we soon got rid of the few possessions we had been using the last two years, and after saying tearful farewells to all our family, relatives, and friends in both Ohio and Pennsylvania, off we went to the *Evangelical Bible Mission Campground and Mission Headquarters at Summerfield, Florida! W*e would be spending the summer there before leaving for *New Guinea* in August of 1969.

WHAT in the world is this that we are about to do? *WHERE is it* that we are about to go? Are we *really ready* to go so far away—*HALFWAY AROUND THE WORLD? HOW LONG* would we stay there before coming back home again? All these questions were being processed in our hearts and minds during our stay at the Mission Headquarters. This *had to be* God's choice for us—not ours*,* otherwise our hearts would not—and could not—be at peace about it. Thankfully, though, God *did* give us that peace. What a blessing that was!

During those months, from June to August, we were kept busy helping with numerous jobs at the campground, and at the same time getting acquainted with the people who lived there and supported the work of Evangelical Bible Mission. Together Daniel and I put shingles on the new roof of the tabernacle. We also did some painting, cleaned the missionary apartment, etc, etc.—whatever needed to be done that we were able to do. Finally, by the end of August, we had our five drums of used clothing and personal goods packed and ready to be shipped by boat, our air-flight was scheduled, and we were ready to head off to the *new world of New Guinea.* Then it was time once again for *good-byes.* This time, however, we were being sent off only by the people at the Mission Headquarters. *No family and no friends from home were there!* Florida was too far away for family and friends at home to come and send us off. They had done that when we first went to Florida! *But now—it was time to be on our way—all the way to New Guinea!* How exciting, yet how we needed the comfort of God's presence going with us all the way to this strange, foreign land—every mile of the way! God's Word provided that comfort and encouragement, and we rested totally on His *promises* as well as His *commission* to the task we were going there to fulfill.

The original tabernacle at Evangelical Bible Mission
Headquarters, at Summerfield, FL

ABOVE:
The tabernacle with its new
roof, where Daniel and I put
on the new shingles in the
summer of 1969

LEFT:
Daniel and I as we were in
the summer of 1969 at the
EBM Headquarters at
Summerfield, FL, just before
leaving USA to go
to New Guinea.

Mark 16:15: *"Go ye into all the world, and preach the gospel to every creature." Matthew 28:20: "Teaching them to observe all things whatsoever I have commanded you."*

"LET'S REACH THEM AND TEACH THEM"

There's many a lad so scantily clad
Along each village road;
If we could just teach them,
I'm sure we could reach them,
And lead them to our God.

And there's many a youth—out of school of a truth,
But now they are standing idle;
What a challenge to reach them,
Though our high school—and teach them
God's Word—the Holy Bible.

There's many a pastor—and what a disaster…
That they can't even read God's Word!
The Gospel has reached them,
But now we must teach them
To study the ways of the Lord.

Then there are fathers and mothers,
And sisters and brothers,
Still living in darkness out there;
Through our pastors we reach them,
Then they'll try to teach them,
As we hold them up in prayer.

So please—every day—remember to pray
For us and these people we love;
We're here to reach them,
To train and to teach them
To win OTHERS for our Lord above.
~~Helen M. Glick~~

This poem was written during our first term in New Guinea, after we had seen first-hand the challenge set before us.

Chapter 3

NEW GUINEA—HERE WE COME!

(TO THE OTHER SIDE OF THE WORLD!)

> Jesus … said,
> "All authority in heaven and on earth has been given to me. Therefore go and make disciples of all nations, baptizing them in the name of the Father and of the Son and of the Holy Spirit, and teaching them to obey everything I have commanded you. And surely I am with you always, to the very end of the age."
> Matthew 28:19-20

Our first flight to New Guinea was truly exciting, for though we had flown to the Bahamas and back several times before, *this was different!* There were so many new experiences about to break forth in our lives, and it was all so exhilarating and exciting, to say the least!

From Orlando, Florida, we went first to Los Angeles, California. On Friday evening, August 22, 1969, just before dark our 747 jet left our homeland, USA, behind us. After making brief stops in *Hawaii* and *Fiji,* as the sun was coming up on Sunday morning at *Sydney, Australia,* our plane came in for another landing. The *time in Sydney* was *19 hrs. ahead* of the *time in Los Angeles*, so after being on the plane 14 hours—mostly in darkness, and having crossed the international date-line, Saturday was already past, and now it was Sunday! How confused we were! Was it *really* time to begin a new day? For the first time we were experiencing what it meant to have *jet-lag!* We were truly weary from travel by then, and even though we had a *long night* to sleep on the plane, we were ready for a good night's sleep *in a bed!*

Since Earl Adams, (Chairman of the Evangelical Bible Mission Board) had preceded us in flight to New Guinea, he had arranged for missionary friends of his in Sydney to meet us at the airport. They took us to their home for rest, sleep, and refreshment until time for our next flight out of Australia to New Guinea the following day. Our host and hostess soon kindly showed us to a room where we slept *all day long*—that is, until their *tea-time.* (We soon learned that *tea-time* in Australia was equivalent to our evening mealtime at home, for it was a *full meal* that they served us when we awoke!) Then, when *their* bedtime came, we were still wide awake and not ready to sleep again. As a result, I spent most of that night reading <u>Head-hunter's Bride</u>, a book which I found lying in the bedroom. *(What a book to read as an introduction to life in New Guinea!)* However, as the night passed, I finally did fall asleep again and slept until time to get up for our departure—first to *Brisbane,* Australia, and then on to *Port Moresby,* the Capital City of New Guinea.

Although we were getting closer to our final destination, we still had two more flights after reaching Port Moresby. From there we would fly to *Mt. Hagen,* in the *Highlands* of New Guinea, and finally the last flight (on a small MAF plane) would take us to *Tambul*—the mission station where we would be living. We expected to be there before the end of the day on Monday; however, an unexpected delay occurred which kept that from happening, so it was not until Tuesday, the *fifth* day after we had left USA that we *finally* reached our new home! That good, long, sleep in Sydney was surely a blessing to our weary bodies as we continued our journey to its end.

EXPERIENCING CULTURE SHOCK

Not only did our overnight experience in Sydney introduce us to some new ways of life as it is lived in the *land down under* (Australia), but also upon reaching Port Moresby, the *vast differences of life in New Guinea* began to emerge right at the airport!

It was a small airport, crowded with multi-racial people, most of whom we had never seen the likes of before—from their physical appearance, their clothes, their language, and everything about them. Even the porters at the airport were dressed with what appeared to be *short, knee-length skirts* rather than trousers. We did not know then what they were called, but later learned that they were *laplaps*—simply a loin cloth wrapped around their body and fastened at the waist. Women wore them, too, though they were longer—down to the ankles. As we went from the international part of the airport to the domestic section where our next flight would take us into the Highlands, there we saw even more amazing sights that boggled our minds! It was all so strange, yet so interesting! There most of the women were wearing the *laplaps*, with loose-fitting blouses (like a maternity blouse)—which we later found to be called a *meri-blouse*. We also noticed that the women were carrying huge brown bags woven of some kind of rope.

Later we learned that these bags were made of strong, cord-like threads from the sisal plant. In those days they were not colored much, except for some designs made in colors from dye gotten from certain garden plants. (However, now they are made of yarn, with beautiful, colorful designs of all sorts. They even design them with their national flag, the American flag, people's names or other words, etc., all hand-woven with different colors of cord-like thread they make from colored yarn.) These bags are called *string-bags* or *bilums* and are used to carry their babies, their garden produce, or whatever needs to be carried. They are tied together and hung from their heads, down their backs, with

33

the weight resting on their hips. But let me stop here in describing *bilums* and their use—as I'll probably get back later with more about that subject.

When we finally arrived in Mount Hagen, the scene was even more surprising and shocking than what it was in Port Moresby. There we began to see women dressed in laplaps, but *without a blouse at all.* They simply covered their shoulders and the bilums they were carrying with another laplap with two corners tied together at the top of their heads. These women were likely women from the surrounding villages who had come to town for shopping, for there were also other women who were not as bodily-exposed in that same way.

Can you imagine how we were feeling about all these strange sights—and sounds, too? With the even smaller airport at Mt. Hagen being quite crowded, the noise of all the strange voices filled the air, until suddenly we heard the familiar sound of English *addressing us by name!* (Although there may have been other voices in English as well, the sounds of *native languages* and *pidgin* were predominant, and we didn't understand much of anything we were hearing. We didn't know the difference in those languages then, but we soon learned!) It was *Paul Bustin*, the pioneer missionary's son, who was speaking to us. We had known that he and his family were living at the Tambul Station where we would be living, but we were surprised to see him there in Mt. Hagen! We were expecting to fly from Mt. Hagen to Tambul in a small *Missionary Aviation Fellowship* plane, so we did not expect to see anyone *from the Mission* until we got to Tambul. After introducing himself to us, Paul offered to *drive* us to Tambul in his vehicle instead of going by plane. Having already collected all our luggage from the international flight, we were waiting at the MAF hanger when Paul made us this offer.

Finally, with everything loaded in his vehicle, we left the airport, heading towards the town of Mt. Hagen and the *Highlands Highway,* for our 3-hour drive through the high mountains between Mt. Hagen and the EBM Tambul Station. As we went along, we were making small talk, and being aware of the different kind of roads, driving conditions, vehicles, etc. that were so strange to us, I asked, *"Are there many road accidents in these parts?"*

Paul's answer was negative, but almost immediately after that question, out of the shadows of the bush-lined road another vehicle approached us from a partially-hidden crossroad and slammed into our vehicle! What a shock! No one was hurt, but the vehicle was no longer road-worthy to make the trip to Tambul!

Being then already late in the afternoon, it was now too late to go back to the airport and make the flight by plane, so we spent the night at the home of an acquaintance of Paul's there in town. In the morning we were taken back to the airport to go to Tambul by flight after all. Paul remained in town to get his vehicle fixed, so we were alone with the pilot in this small MAF craft!

(I forgot to mention before how amazingly beautiful the skies were, with their fluffy white clouds, when we flew from Port Moresby to Mt. Hagen. Now, on this small MAF plane, flying low, just above the teeming mountains on the way to Tambul, we saw another array of breath-taking beauty. We seemed almost to touch the tops or edges of the mountains as we flew just above the peaks and between the ranges at some places. God's world in New Guinea was so fearfully and wonderfully made, and seeing it from a *heavenly* viewpoint was a marvelous sight of great wonder.)

And so it was, on Tuesday, the 26th of August, 1969, we *finally* ended our last flight on the tiny airstrip at the Tambul Government Station—with the Tambul EBM Mission Station not far away. Can you imagine the mixed emotions that filled our hearts and minds as we got out of the plane? Immediately we were surrounded with black men, women, and children standing there with *Earl Adams*, the *Mission Board Chairman,* who had preceded us to Tambul, and now had come to the airstrip to meet us.

Standing there with Bro. Adams were men, wearing no clothing—except for a loin cloth hanging down the front of their body from under a wide bark belt, and with only clusters of leaves with their stem also tucked under their belt, covering their backside. The women were wearing *nothing but strings* around their waists, with more strings hanging down from their waist to cover their private parts in front and behind. They wore no blouses to cover their bosoms. Of the children, (boys and girls alike) many were practically naked. They wore *only a few strings* around their waists and hanging down their front and back—which only partially covered the nakedness of their little bodies. I cannot fully remember all the emotions I felt at that time, but I can almost feel fresh, unbelievable, shocking ones rising up within me now as I write this, realizing again how surprising it would be for *anyone* raised in a culture like our own to face such circumstances for the first time! If it would happen here in USA, you would almost think you had inadvertently just arrived at a nudist camp hidden back in the bush somewhere! But for there, all this was normal!

Oh, *how good is our GOD*, to provide all the grace and support needed for those shocking experiences, and for those that were yet to come! Only *HE* could provide comfort and strength for such times as these, being so far away from friends and family! The strangeness of it all was overwhelming!

OUR NEW HOME at EBM'S TAMBUL STATION

So...here we were at the *Tambul Government Station,* located in the flat Tambul Valley at the foot of *Mt. Gilowe*—a mountain reaching to the height of *14,000 feet*. The valley itself lies at an elevation of 7,500 ft. with a pass of more than 8,000 ft. to cross when going to Mt. Hagen—a three-hour drive away. All our shopping would be done there. The ride to the *Tambul Mission Station* from the Government Station, however, was not far at all—possibly only a mile. As we drove into the station, we were surprised at the beauty of what we saw there, in contrast to the Government Station. On the right near the entrance, there was a small store. Then the road through the station was lined on the right with huge, majestic, green bamboo trees, and the lawns beyond them were gorgeously fresh and green as well. Flowers lined the left side of the road, as well as a small ditch flowing with crystal clear water. A boys' dormitory—with a bush house behind it, and three well-built wood-framed missionary houses were spread out along the left side of the road. The lovely brown-trimmed white house in the middle was going to be our new home, and how anxious we were to get inside and take a look!

Also on the right side of the road, a large, three-room school-house and a *huge* tabernacle were sitting back from the road in the midst of the beautiful green lawn. In that same lawn, nearer to the road, was a large gold-fish pond surrounding the island of flowers in the middle of it. Further on, near the end of the station, (on the right side) there was a large, thatch-covered workshop and some small bush dwellings for station workers. From there, the road became a footpath leading down to a river with a 2-log bridge for crossing the swift-flowing river below. From there the footpath continued on to five villages that formed a half-circle reaching to the farthest stretch of the valley in the middle and then back again to Tambul at the other end. These villages were the location of some of EBM's *Tambul-Outstations,* where many Christians came to worship in small bush-churches.

Oh, but I must move on! There's so much to tell you, so I must cut out some of the details! After having lived at Andros Island in the Bahamas, the house we were now moving into was simply *fantastically beautiful* and *luxurious* in comparison! It was built from lumber cut out from the mountain and crafted by an earlier missionary. Now we were having the privilege of living there! I felt like we were living in a mansion! My white nylon

Priscilla curtains stretched across the three joined windows at the front of the house making it like a large picture window!

All the furniture was home-made, with foam cushions for the chairs and couch in the living room and also a 4-inch foam for a mattress on the flat, wooden bed. We even had an indoor bathroom, as the water ran by gravity from the huge water tank that sat up on stilts in the back of the house to catch the rain from the roof. For a shower, we had a large galvanized bucket with a shower-rose fastened on the bottom. A rope and pulley were used to pull the bucket full of water above our heads when we would take our showers. One bucket full did the job nicely! There was, however, no water heater, so if the water was not warm enough from being in the sunshine all day, then a bit of hot water heated on a little wooden stove in the living room could be added to give enough warmth for a comfortable shower.

One end of the living room was covered with built-in bookshelves. That was so handy, and it made the room look homey! The house also had a small utility closet, a small office, a small storage room, and three bedrooms—besides the kitchen, dining area, living room and the bathroom. I would say that is quite an extraordinary house for on a mission field, wouldn't you? At least that is what we thought, and *we were so thankful for it.*

(The earlier missionaries, who had first lived in bush houses, had done all the work that made this comfort possible for us. Living there would now be so much easier for us—especially compared to what we had experienced in the Bahama Islands. We deeply appreciated all the hard work past missionaries had done to make living there at Tambul more comfortable and enjoyable!)

Well ... so much for the house that would be our new home! That was *not* as important as our *purpose* for being there. The Paul Bustin family lived in the house next to ours toward the end of the station, but they would soon be leaving. We were there to fill the vacancy they would leave behind. Besides them, the *Hollingsworths* lived in the first house, toward the entrance of the station. They were an older couple who had come to help in the work there for two years, so it was not long after we came that they also left and returned to USA. While there, *Sister Hollingsworth (as we called each other Bro. and Sister)* worked mostly with the ladies, teaching them the Gospel, how to sew, etc., but she also taught Bible lessons to children as well. *Bro. Hollingsworth* worked as a general handyman, repairman, and gardener on the station. Their house-girl, *Mindilik*, was a teenage girl, but she often served as an interpreter for them (and also for us) because she could speak both English and *Pidgin*—as well as her own tribal language.

NEW GUINEA LANGUAGES: PIDGIN / TOKPLES

Pidgin is the trade-language spoken throughout the country. For most people, it is easy to learn and to understand. Missionaries usually become fluent in the use of the *Pidgin* language and enjoy speaking it even amongst themselves. It consists of simplified forms of English words spelled phonetically, German words, and words from the coastal tribal languages. Here is an example of a familiar Bible verse as it is written in the Pidgin Bible, (which is called *BUK BAIBEL.*)

~~Jon 3:16~~
"God I gat wanpela Pikinini tasol I stap.
Tasol God I laikim tumas olgeta manmeri bilong graun,
olsem na em I givim dispela wanpela Pikinini long ol.
Em I mekim olsem
bilong olgeta manmeri I bilip long em
ol I no ken lus. Nogat.
Bai ol I kisim laip I stap gut oltaim oltaim."

Now, here is a little lesson in the *Pidgin* language.
(Have Fun!)
1. <u>The vowels are pronounced as in Spanish—</u>
<u>not as in English.</u>

A = ah, E = a, I = e, O = oh, U = oo
Thus—the word for *eye* sounds much like English,
but it is spelled *"ai,"*
and the words for *me* and *you* are spelled *"mi"* and *"yu"*!

2. <u>Here are the meanings of some of the main words</u>
<u>used in the verse above:</u>

a. Pikinini – son
b. tasol – only / but
c. olgeta – all
d. bilong graun – on earth
e. oltaim oltaim – everlasting (forever and ever)
f. mekim olsem – did this
g. no ken lus – will not perish
h. kisim laip – will get life
I. gat – has
j. wanpela – one
k. bilip – believe

l. manmeri – people
m. Em – He
n. dispela – this
o. givim – gave
p. laikim tumas – loves
q. olsem na – therefore
r. long ol – to them
s. I stap – is (the verb "to be")

Now, read the verse in Pidgin again, and see if it makes a
bit more sense to you!

It may also interest you to know that throughout the country there are *more than* 700 *distinct tribal languages,* but *few* missionaries learn any of these languages fluently unless they are working with Bible translation, in health clinics, etc. Many Bible Translators have been busy working in *all* parts of the country for many years to translate the Bible into *all* these different languages. At any given place, the tribal language of that particular area is referred to in Pidgin as *tokples*—the *talk of the place*. In many provinces, all communication among the people themselves is done in their tribal *tokples*—especially in the village setting. However, Pidgin is also the common language used in many churches, newspapers, government meetings, places of business, radio programming, etc. all throughout the country.

OK! Enough about the languages in New Guinea!
I hope you had a bit of fun with that lesson!

Our lovely home at the EBM Tambul Station
where we lived during most of our first term
in New Guinea—Aug. 1969 - Dec. 1973

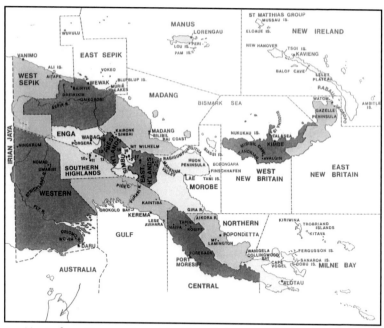

Most of our time and work in New Guinea was in the Western & Southern Highlands Provinces—except for Port Moresby & Lae.

A typical, newly-planted kaukau (sweet potato) garden

Chapter 4

OUR LIFE and WORK at TAMBUL

The Tambul Station had 18 outstations* where there were small bush churches and native Christian men who were serving as pastors. One of Daniel's responsibilities was to have a weekly Bible study class for these pastors. This was no easy task—especially until we learned to speak *Pidgin*. Most of the village people and many of the pastors spoke *only tokples* (their local tribal language). They did not know how to *speak* Pidgin, though some could *partially understand* it. That meant that the translation had to be done twice. First, Daniel would speak in English, and whoever was available that could understand both English and Pidgin would translate it into Pidgin. Then one of the pastors who understood Pidgin would translate the lesson again into *tokples*.

~~~~~~~~~

*Here is a list of the names of the 18 Tambul Outstations:
(You might like to try pronouncing them!)
Kikuwa, Kuliana, Kulipena, Lamidi, Tope, Liakame, Malke, Moka, Opiyepulu, Kondipi, Karawi, Akepagi, Pukumuka, Lomogopulu, Talpica, Marapulu, Tomba, Wapokolia.

~~~~~~~~~

Besides teaching the pastors and visiting outstation churches, Daniel was also the *Station Manager*—which included managing the station's large 90 acre farm. There were many acres of garden produce growing there to be marketed in Mt. Hagen. At that time, the produce being marketed included: carrots, cabbage, cauliflower, turnips, parsnips, potatoes, beets, broccoli, and strawberries. Sweet potatoes, the staple food of all the highlands people, were also grown in abundance on the station. Later on, the number of cattle on the farm was increased to 15, utilizing more of the areas that were not suitable for farming. The cattle could roam throughout the uneven terrain and get their water supply from the river that flowed through the more distant parts of the station.

As for me, it did not take long for me to know what the Lord wanted me to be doing there. Very shortly after our arrival, two little girls (one completely bald) came knocking at our back verandah door. Their question was spoken in simple English that could easily be understood, and my heart was deeply moved.

"Will you be our teacher?" they pleaded eagerly.

I cannot recall now just how I answered them, but I knew immediately that this was the task the Lord had waiting for me to do.

As it was, I learned later that their Government-registered school on the Mission Station had been closed down because their previous young, single missionary teacher had forsaken her classes and was spending her time with a young, *Australian* male *Agriculture Department* worker at the Government Station. She was still in the area when we arrived, but we never saw her nor met her before she finally left the area altogether. Therefore, the children who had attended the school on the station were now without anyone to teach them, and they wanted their classes to be started up again. The school year would be ending in December, so there were not many months left to the present school year; nevertheless, our arrival gave them hope that the school would soon be opened up again.

My experiences of teaching school at Peniel, in OH and at the school on the campgrounds in PA now began to make a lot more sense. At those schools I had taught students of different ages—grades 1-5, and then high school—*all without credentials.* And now, even in New Guinea (for lack of those credentials) I would not be able to teach in an *accredited school*, such as the school had been before it was closed. However, all those previous experiences would *help to prepare me* for what I was about to begin there at Tambul—in spite of the lack of credentials. Instead of having an *accredited* school, we would start what would be called the *Tambul Bible Center*.

Nevertheless, there would still be a great difference in teaching in New Guinea from what I had done before, and I felt completely unprepared on my own to tackle this new challenge! If I were to fulfill the request of those little girls, *I definitely had to have special help from the Lord for the task.* (You see, these children were being *taught in English* at school, even though they knew none of the language when they first came to school! Their lessons were pre-planned and prepared in a syllabus from the Australian Education Department, using a method that helped the students to learn the English as they were being taught everything else. *But I had no such syllabus to guide me, or any other materials to use for any of the subjects they had been learning.* The young teacher who had been teaching them had borrowed the syllabus and other materials she used from the Government School, and she had returned them. *Now—how was I to handle this call for help from these needy children?*)

As I had done many times before, I made this perplexing situation a matter of special prayer. It was then that I realized that God was leading me to visit *the Kauapena Station*—another of the EBM Stations in the Highlands—where there was a large, thriving accredited school and excellent missionary teachers. *Betty Congrove* was the teacher I went to visit. During that visit, Betty helped me tremendously by explaining to me their teaching system. She also gave me some materials that I would need. I then went back to the Tambul Government School, and was again allowed to borrow the Australian syllabus which I needed for the task. In addition, in order build up a library of other necessary books, I went to the bookstore in Mt. Hagen and bought the books and supplies that were needed. All this was taking place in the month of September, so that by the beginning of October all was ready to re-open a class for the 40 students of *Standards* 1 and 2 (*Grades* 1 & 2) to complete the 1969 school year in December! How motivated I was, and what a thrill it was to give all my time and energy to preparing to teach these dear children—*not for a paycheck*—but for the *LORD* alone!

(Actually, finances were not a predominant concern for us, because our service for the Lord in New Guinea was not based on what we would be receiving in monetary support, but on *what the Lord was giving us to do*. Our support was based on what the Lord would provide for us from month to month. When we had left our home church in Ohio, our Pastor told us that our home church congregation wanted to help us with this need. [They had not done that when we went to the Bahamas in 1963.] The amount suggested to him that we would need each month was $80.00 each. That meant we would be receiving $160.00 for the two of us each month from our church. Other than that, we had no *promise* of any support, except that we were still getting our check of $100 each month for the sale of our house in Michigan ten years before! *[You see, God had a long-range plan for the sale of that house—which we didn't know about then! How wonderful is the wisdom of our God!]* Consequently, month by month God provided for *all* our personal needs. Financial needs for the school were provided by what was produced on the station from the gardens and the little trade-store.)

I do not know how things were before we went there, but we soon found out that many of the children had a long way to walk to come to school, so we arranged for them to stay on the station during the week days and go home to their villages over the weekends. The boys used the dorm building near the entrance of the station for sleeping, and cooked their own sweet potatoes in the ashes of a fire they built in the bush *cook-house* behind the dorm. At first there was no dormitory for the girls, so they used one of the three classrooms in the school building as their dorm. A small grass hut nearby was their place for making fire and cooking their food. Sweet potatoes (called *kaukau* in Pidgin) could be cooked almost anywhere a fire could be built to make hot ashes. No pan or any kind of utensil was needed, and they even scraped the skin from their *kaukau* with a sharpened edge of a piece of bamboo instead of using a knife. Then they would bury the *kaukau* in the hot ashes and leave it there until it was tender enough to be eaten. Later Daniel built a nice dormitory for the girls which also included a place for them to prepare their food as well.

As for washing up, the children would dip in the cool stream of water in the ditch that ran through the station along the road, so they pretty much took care of themselves.

By God's help, that first segment of teaching was completed in December with a break until late January or early February when the next school year would begin. It was so wonderful that words cannot adequately express the joy I had just to be there teaching those precious children!

As we prepared to begin another full school year, we also opened up the way for a new class of students. These children would be younger, and many would not know English or Pidgin—only their local tribal language. However, the Lord provided for us a well-qualified national teacher, *Kakaiye,** (from the Kauapena Station) who would be working with these children on a Prep level. She could communicate with them in *tokples*, and also with us in both English and Pidgin.

~~~~~~~~~~~~~~~~~~~~~~

*(In June of 2011 we received news that Kakaiye had a stroke and has gone to be with the Lord Jesus. We praise God for our good memories of her, and for her service as a teacher at Tambul Bible Center many years ago.)

When the children came to our house to register for the new school year, we would give them a small set of clothing. To the boys we gave a shirt and pair of short pants, and to the girls we gave a small meri-blouse and a skirt. Usually the girls came with their tribal clothing of strings for a skirts—with no blouses, and the boys would be wearing leaves and a small loincloth in place of trousers. One little boy, however, presented himself for registration in his *birthday suit*—that is, completely naked!

The final new class for 1970 numbered another 40 children. Some of these students would stay on the station with the previous students, but not all of them. Only those from a long distance would remain on the station until the weekends and then go home.

~~~~~~~~~~~~~~~~~~~~~~~~~~~~~~~

Now I want to pause here in *My Story* to include a three-part article that I had written for the *Mission Messenger* (EBM's Missionary publication) in the months of September, October, and November of 1970. As you read each *Part*, I hope you will imagine that you were there, seeing and hearing all that took place at that time. I hope your heart will be moved as mine was while re-reading it! What a joy it was to serve God in this way, and in this place, planting the seed of God's Word in the hearts and lives of precious children who might have otherwise never had such an opportunity to be taught about Jesus. For such a time as this, God had placed us there to fulfill our assignment of being His witnesses to these children—as well as adults. And perhaps He is calling *you* just now, to follow Him and be His witness at a specific place and in a special way that He has designed for you. *Fear not! Be His faithful servant! (Isaiah 41:10)*

A TYPICAL TUESDAY at TAMBUL

(Part I)

Ri-i-n-g! Oh, it's six o'clock already! How the time does fly! It was the alarm in the girls' dorm that I had just heard. For the past half hour I had been in the classroom right next to the dorm, preparing the blackboards for the day's classes. I had had my devotions earlier, and now the girls were having theirs. Just a few minutes after the alarm went off, I heard them singing—quite sleepily at first. I peeked into the room and saw them sitting on their grass-filled ticks, which were side by side on the floor; they were snugly wrapped in their blankets to keep warm. After singing their songs, some in Pidgin and some in English, they quietly listened as their house-mother read to them from her *Nupela Testamen.* This was followed by an exhortation in their native language, and then there was a chorus of voices as they all began to pray. It all sounded like music to my ears, and I thanked the Lord for providing us with a good house-mother for the girls.

Before long the girls came out of their dorm room, one by one, heading for the kitchen. It would be warm there, and all were anxious for that warmth, even though their breakfast of kaukau (sweet potatoes) would not be ready yet. The cook would be there in the kitchen preparing it over the open fire.

By now it was 6:30, time for me to go quickly to the house to get our own breakfast. It was Tuesday, and at seven we should be finished with all our personal morning activities. I'd have to hurry back after breakfast, too, for the blackboard work for the three classes was not finished, and I really wasn't ready for the school day to begin yet.

Oh, how nice and cozy it was in the house. Daniel had started the fire in the living room stove, and there he was, sitting near the stove having his morning devotions. As I went to the kitchen, I heard someone cough out on the back porch.

"Oh, no," I thought, *"Not already!"*

Taking a look, I saw what I expected. Someone was there with a bag of kaukau, waiting for Daniel to start buying. The cough was their way of letting us know they were there.

"They'll just have to wait," I said to myself. "It's not seven yet." Quickly I prepared breakfast and called Daniel.

By the time we finished eating and had prayer together, the crowd at the back of the house had increased greatly. All were waiting with loaded bags to sell their kaukau. (One lady's bag had 50 lbs. of potatoes in it!) For the next hour or more Daniel was busy buying kaukau from the people. He would take it along to town that afternoon or the next day. 500 pounds would be sold to the Boys' Technical School in Mt. Hagen, and what remained would be sold at the market. For the local people this was an opportunity to make a few extra shillings, and they all clamored for it. However, Daniel finally had to appoint certain villages to come at certain times, for they were bringing more than we could buy at one time.

While Daniel was busy weighing and buying the kaukau, I slipped out the front door to take up where I left off in the classrooms. By this time the school children were seen here and there around the station, and over near the ditch of running water where they were getting their morning bath. With their towels lying on the ground nearby, some could be seen standing in the stream in the process of dousing their heads in the cold water. Then they applied the soap and began to wash their hair, face, arms, hands, legs, and feet—with their clothes on. Others already finished were walking back to their dorms with their towels thrown on top of their heads. What an interesting sight to behold! But—that's the way they always do their washing up! They don't know anything about using warm water. (When at their villages, the nearest river is their bathing place as well as the place they get their drinking water, too.)

Then I left off watching the children and went into my classroom. Eight o'clock would come soon enough! Already some of the children gathered around the schoolhouse, still eating and carrying in their hands some of their breakfast of kaukau. Very soon it would be time for the first bell.

(To Be Continued)

Preparing one of the blackboards for the day's school work. This work is for the Standard I students.

Daniel and one of the workers buying the Kaukau on our back porch. Women carry these bags, some containing as much as 50 pounds suspended from their heads. The girls learn very young to carry loads this way. Babies are carried this way, too.

Above: Praying the Lord's Prayer in the morning line-up

Some of the girls in their dorm during morning devotion time. Sixteen school girls and their housemother sleep in this large room.

That article you've just read gives you a brief glimpse of the early years of our life in New Guinea at the Tambul Station. But let me continue on with *Part II* of that article. It says so much that it would be hard for me to describe in another way about what life was like there. Remember, however, that it is describing the activities of just *one day out of seven* in a week's time! So now, please read on…

A TYPICAL TUESDAY at TAMBUL
(Part II)

Stand at ease! Attention! Right dress! Eyes front! Forward dress! Hands down! Yes, it's eight o'clock, and there they are—all lined up in straight lines—just like little soldiers. They've sung their National Anthem, and now they stand with bowed heads, praying the Lord's Prayer. In just a moment they will be checked for cleanliness before marching to their classes.

Since there aren't any announcements, the Prep class is quickly checked and told to march to their class. Their teacher is waiting for them in her classroom on the large platform of the tabernacle. For the first hour (or nearly so) all 46 Prep students are together for a time of singing and Scripture memorization in addition to Bible lessons in their own language. Then half of them are dismissed and will return for their lessons in English later in the day.

But now—back to those standing in the line. Some of them are missing, it seems. Oh, I see them now. They are over by the water ditch, washing their hands. Pillowa and Liye are racing towards the dorm. They've been told to put on clean shirts. (It seems the children's standard of cleanliness in not quite the same as ours, but they do quite well, considering everything. We appreciate the progress they are making along this line.) With all back in line again, Standard II is now ready to march into its classroom.

During all this time, I am only an observer, for one of the older Standard III students takes care of the line-up procedures. Now it is time for me to get into my classroom. But first, there is the work assignment for Standard III students. On Tuesday, work-time is devoted to various jobs around the station. Today there's weeding to be done in the strawberries, but sometimes they clean flower beds, cut grass, clean water ditches, pick up stones, or just anything that needs to be done. They will work until recess time, then after recess they will come to the classroom for a class before Chapel time.

Having the blackboards all ready with the written lessons of the day helps the day to move along more smoothly. While Class A is doing written work, Class B has their oral lessons. Then while Class A is having oral lessons, Class B writes. Every spare moment is used to check their work or put new lessons on the board for the next day. There are daily lessons in spelling, writing, reading, arithmetic, written sentences, and composition (oral and written). Natural science is taught on Tuesday, health on Wednesday, and social studies whenever it can be worked in. On Thursday the girls have sewing class while the boys work at a garden project. 10:00 a.m. and 2:30 p.m. are recess times, and at 11:15 it's Chapel time. We'll tell you more about Chapel time later. Now, while the children are in their kitchens eating their lunch of kaukau, let's go look for Daniel. It's time for our lunch, too. Kinie, my house-girl, has prepared some fresh vegetable soup with vegetables from our garden and some we bought from the local people. A tin of canned meat adds some flavor, too. This is a treat for Kinie, for usually her meals consist of kaukau only. She eats with us at noon each day, though. Oh, there's Daniel. He just came out of the tabernacle. He's been working in there lately. (The two classrooms he's building in the back are coming along nicely now. Soon he'll be ready for the concrete to do the floors.)

"Will you soon be ready for lunch, Daniel?" I called.

"Not just yet—you go ahead! I have something to do in the shop," he answered.

In the house Kinie had been doing some mending for some of the workers throughout the morning. She also straightened the house and washed the dishes. In the afternoon she will sew up some more lap-laps for the store. (Lap-laps are straight pieces of cloth [about 60 inches long], hemmed at each end and used as a wrap-around skirt or in place of trousers.) She now has the table all set and ready for lunch. While waiting for Daniel I check on things around the house. But I see it is already 12:45, so I must go ahead and eat. Daniel still didn't come. However, just as Kinie and I sat down, Daniel came. By the time he got washed and ready to eat, it was time for me to run along to school again. Therefore, a few hasty words are all Daniel and I could share at this time.

The afternoon line-up is quickly formed, and after only brief procedures, all march into their classes again. Now the second group of prep students will have their classes. Standard II has classes until recess; afterwards they will go to the garden to pick the strawberries for market. Standard III students now continue their lessons during the rest of the afternoon—sometimes it's five o'clock before we're finished.

Going back to the house, I find Kinie still working in the sewing room. Mindilk is there, too. She is finishing the ironing which she started the day before. She goes to the government school, so has only a little time in the evenings to do her work. (She often serves as interpreter for us in our services as well.)

Daniel is in the shop now helping to get the picked strawberries arranged in the big box to take them to market. The 2,000 pounds of kaukau which he has bought from Christian people is bagged and weighed and is ready to be loaded on Goriye's truck. He will take the things to market very early in the morning. Besides the kaukau and strawberries, there are a few turnips and tomatoes. The lettuce and carrots from the children's project garden will wait until Saturday when Daniel goes to market again.

Our supper of hamburgers, lettuce and tomatoes, green beans, and potatoes is ready and waiting. It's seven o'clock, but Daniel is still out in the shop. Tonight there are some good letters to share with him, for Mindilk brought some from the Post Office when she came home from school. How good it is to receive your friendly and encouraging letters. When the day's labors are ended, it is good to know that someone has been standing by us in this quiet way.

As you see, not all our labors are in ministering directly to the spiritual needs of those about us. There is much more involved in missionary work than this, though this truly is our aim, purpose, and goal. It is the most glorious part of our work, too, for it leaves us with a sense of having shared with our people the richest of all treasures known to mankind. I have not yet spoken of this part of our day, but in the next writing I'll tell you about it. Chapel time is that part of the day when my heart is overflowing with joy for the privilege of having such a group of boys and girls to whom I can teach God's Word. It makes the rest of the time spent in the classrooms seem worthwhile. The *grace of God* has been abundantly sufficient as we try our best to keep the school running smoothly. We marvel how He has seen us through several critical times when our help was decreased, but we feel it has been for the best in each case. We have seen again and again how *"All things work together for good to them that love God, to them who are the called according to His purpose." (Romans 8:28)* For this we praise our Wonderful God!

(To be continued)

Wow! Are you tired, yet? *At this stage of my life,* just re-reading about the full schedule of activities for one day makes me tired just to remember it all! In those days, both Daniel and I had *lots of energy,* and we were in good health. How we thank the Lord for those blessings, which helped to make the beginning years of our life there in New Guinea rich and full and satisfying! But now, there's one more part to that article *A Typical Tuesday at Tambul* that I also want to include, so here it is—read on, and may you be blessed as you imagine yourself there with us!

A TYPICAL TUESDAY at TAMBUL
Part III
CHAPEL TIME

"Gospel Bells are ringing in the Chapel,
They're ringing out the message of God's love;
We want to win for Jesus all our children,
And take them with us to our home above."

Not only on Tuesdays, but EVERY day of the school week the entire student body gathers in the large tabernacle for Chapel-time. I can see them now—all lined up outside and ready to march in. And now, there they go—singing their favorite marching song: *"1 - 2 – 3 – Jesus Died for Me!"* If you could see all their happy, smiling faces and hear their lusty voices as they heartily join in the singing, your heart would be thrilled.

There are many songs they love to sing—all in English. A few they know in both English and Pidgin, and these are hardly well sung unless they've been sung in both languages. A couple of the songs are also sung in their local native language as well as in English. Next it's prayer time. Daily our prayers ascend with thanksgiving for guidance, help, and victory in our Chapel-time, as well as for the needs of others. Some of the children who are Christians share in these times of prayer by praying aloud in their own native language or in Pidgin. Most would find it too difficult to pray in English.

After this, sometimes there are testimonies, but more frequently the children share with others the Bible verses they've learned. Just this week my heart was tremendously overjoyed as we daily listened to the children one by one saying all their memory verses for the study of the book of *Genesis*, which we completed during the last term.

Among the things the children bring to Chapel-time are their folders containing colorful circles with their memory verses printed on them. The theme for the *Genesis* study was *"God is Calling Us."* A huge telephone was used on the flannel-board, and as each new verse was presented, a circle with the verse printed on it

56

was placed on the dial. Likewise, on the front of their memory-verse folders is a large telephone reminding them that God is personally calling each one of them.

Having already learned the *Books of the Bible*, I felt the children were now ready to use a Bible themselves. Therefore, we purchased 20 Bibles to give out as rewards for correctly saying all 15 of their verses at one standing. While each one recited, the others quietly followed their folders and listened for the verse to be said correctly. Only three of the 19 who already received their Bibles needed a little extra time to study a few of the verses again. And how happy they were to receive a Bible of their own! Just today another order was prepared for more so that the rest can receive theirs, too.

After all the Standard I, II, and III children have learned their verses, (and a few Prep students are nearly ready to say them all, too), I also want to help them understand each verse well, so they can give its meaning to their family and friends. Thus they can help *ring the Gospel Bells* in their villages, too!

Next year the *Genesis* lessons will be followed by another flannel-graph series on the book of *Exodus*. These lessons should prove more meaningful to the children as they follow the stories in their Bibles. Also, while we are reviewing our Genesis lessons this term, with the use of their Bibles, we shall teach some new lessons from the *Psalms* and the *New Testament*, too. Beginning next week we will be learning about the *23rd Psalm*.

Words cannot express the thankfulness I feel in my heart for the privilege of teaching our children these wonderful lessons. The promise is that *God's Word* will not return void, so *by His help* we want to be faithful in giving out *the TRUTH that will mold these young lives for an eternity with Christ in Heaven.*

Another thing that brings joy to our hearts is to see our children bow at an altar and pray, as some have done on occasions. Many of them are very young in their *faith*, and it is now our duty to nurture them in the good things of God; and since we believe the study of God's Word and hiding it in one's heart will accomplish this more quickly than anything else, we therefore labor to this end.

I cannot close this writing about Chapel-time without mentioning our *Religious Instruction Class* at the local government school. (Such a class was permitted in all government schools, to be taught by any missions in the area who cared to use this time.) Though this class comes only once a week, it is a blessed privilege to give these same lessons to boys and girls of Catholic and Lutheran backgrounds (who come to the class), as well as to those from our own EBM Outstation Churches. These children are also learning the same Bible verses, though we have not yet finished the series of lessons on *Genesis*. We aim to finish this series by the end of this school year.

Their Catholic head-teacher, upon seeing a memory-verse folder on a student's desk, and after having read the verse from *John 10:9*, began to question the student about who said those words. When the student replied that Jesus did, he then asked why John's name was thus attached to the verse. Then the student again answered well, for he told how that Jesus said the words, but John wrote them down. Satisfied that the student answered well, the teacher commended him for knowing the meaning, and not just having the folder with Bible verses for nothing.

This little incident is a challenge to me. Please help us pray for this head-teacher and his co-worker, for I believe God's Word is able to reach them for the Lord, too.

We shall keep ringing the Gospel Bells as long as we can, that others can be prepared to continue ringing them when we are called to move on. Please continue to pray for us, as you have been. We appreciate the prayers of each of you. God bless you!

THE END
(*Mission Messenger* articles, Sept. - Nov., 1970)

~~~~~~~~~~~~~~~~~~~~

Oh! How I loved all those children! Words cannot describe the joy in my heart to be able to share with them not only their lessons from the syllabus, but also the Bible Lesson series being taught to them in their Chapel-time. As time went on, some of them became ardent believers in the Lord Jesus Christ as their Savior.* *Oh, how I praise the Lord for every one of them who sooner or later took that step of faith for their own personal Salvation!*

*(One outstanding example of a student coming to faith in the Lord Jesus during our chapel time was *Pyongo*. He was a boy of Catholic background from another area, who was living with one of the local-area students and began coming to our school. On the day that he responded to the gospel message and came for prayer, I was truly overjoyed. As he stood to give a brief testimony after praying, the Lord laid him on my heart and said to me, "*Here is a new-born babe-in-Christ whom I want you to nurture and care for like a son.*" From that point on I did all I could to encourage his spiritual growth and development—including writing many letters to him for quite a few years after he moved to another area, went to another school, and finally graduated from high school in his home town of Mendi. I still count him as one of my *special sons* to this day.)

LEFT: Milo Timini (A special helper whom I mentored like a "son")
RIGHT: Andrew Pyongo (My "son" in the faith)

The 1970 school year was completed with me still being the only teacher for the first class of students now being divided into Standards I, II, and III. When 1971 came, we took in a second group of new prep students. But having teachers for all the original 1970 classes now became a major concern. Nevertheless, with the help of one of my older students, and a new missionary teacher—

Esther Hershey, we managed to continue through the second full year of 1971. In August of that year, however, another surprising development occurred that brought new life into our family picture and changed a lot of things!

Kinie—our faithful house girl

Tambul School Children in our home

Chapter 5

ADDING "JOY" to OUR HOME

It all began when a crying baby was brought to the back verandah of our house by three people from one of the villages of the Tambul Valley that was most distant from the mission station. The baby's mother had hung herself four days earlier, leaving her 8½-month-old child in the *bilum* (string bag), in which she carried her about from place to place. The bilum was hanging against the wall inside the house with the crying baby inside. The relatives who brought her said the child had been crying for four days and would not eat anything they offered her—namely, *kaukau* (sweet potatoes—which is their staple food). No one was available to nurse her, and she would not be satisfied with anything else! The relatives actually thought she was going to die, for they didn't know how to get her to stop crying. When they brought her to us, the father was at home with her small older brother, grieving and mourning over the loss of his wife.

Thankfully, I happened to remember that I had a baby bottle in my cupboard, so immediately I fixed a bottle of warm milk for the crying baby. When I presented it to her, she reached out her little hands, and grasping the bottle firmly, she drank hungrily. Then the crying stopped immediately, and everyone who brought her was so happy!

But what should we do now? That was the next question! To give the bottle to them would be *an illegal thing to do* since New Guinea women were not permitted to use a bottle without a prescription from the doctor! *Why?* — because in the village setting there were no sanitary conditions to take care of bottles, no refrigeration to keep milk from spoiling, and no place to get a supply of milk! Also, for them it would be much too far to come daily to the mission station to get the milk the baby would need. So…what should we do to help this motherless baby?

As the baby drank contentedly, Daniel and I pondered the situation and talked it over inside the house, trying to decide what to do. As it was, I was so deeply engrossed in my work at the school, and there was no way for me to take on another major responsibility without help! Also, we did not want to keep the child in our home just long enough to get her over the crisis, getting closely attached to her, only to have to give her up again. These were our thoughts on the matter. Finally, we went out again and asked the relatives what they wanted us to do.

Speaking in Pidgin, we said, *"Yupela I tingting wanem? Yupela I laik long mitupela ken kisim em olgeta na lukautim em, o nogat?"* (Translated in English: *"What do you think? Would you like for us to keep her permanently and take care of her?"*)

They all smiled, and in reply, answered with a hearty, *"Tru tumas, supos yutupela I mekin olsem, mipela I gat bikpela amamas tru!"* (Translated, that means, *"Yes, we would really be happy if you would do that!"*)

However, they also said they would need to check first with the father to see how he would feel about letting us keep the child permanently. They agreed to come back and let us know; and with that, they went home, leaving the darling little baby with us. How happy and excited we were! At last we had a small baby to live in our house!

The little one had on no clothes—only a string around her neck. Her village name was *Neka,* but from then on we called her Joy Regina. *JOY*—because she was bringing to us *great joy* to have a baby in our home at this later stage of our lives—(I was 37 and Daniel was 39, and we had been married 18 years by this time!) Then we called her *REGINA,* because that was what we had long ago planned to call our first daughter—whenever that would come to pass!

So, that is how little *Joy Regina* (at 8½ months of age) became a vital part of our lives from that time on! With her, God also gave us a wonderful helper in the person of *Kinie*, a young Bible School student who had completed her studies and who had already been helping me in the home while I was busy in school. From then on, she was daily in the home caring for Joy, baking bread, doing the laundry and house cleaning, mending and sewing for the little trade store, preparing some of our meals, etc. all day long. She was truly God's gift of a wonderful helper for me! In the late afternoons and evenings when both Daniel and I would be in the home again, then together we took over caring for our little bundle of JOY! We were truly happy and rejoicing over God's *gifts* to us.

(Kinie continued as our house-girl during all the time we lived at the Tambul Station, and also served in the same way by helping a number of other missionary families who later lived there. What a blessing she has been to so many of us through the years! Kinie's marriage to John Kili was one of the first of many marriages that Daniel performed while in New Guinea).

I would like to tell you many more details about Joy being a part of our busy life, and about the school at Tambul, but this part of my story would get much too lengthy if I did that. However, I must mention that with each year Joy added great interest and blessing to our family, and everyone loved her! Nevertheless, the growing number of students required more help with the teaching, and after one period of time when I had been teaching two classes in two separate rooms—that is, in the new classrooms Daniel had built in the tabernacle to the right and left of the entrance doors—I was getting quite worn out! As we cried out to the Lord for help, He sent us two young ladies (from two other of our EBM stations) who came to the rescue—*Glowaye* and *Cindy*. Besides them, it was *Esther Hershey*, who had come to us from Ohio in 1971, who helped by teaching the last of the original students all the way through to completing Standard VI, when they were ready to take a high school entrance exam in 1974.

STUDENTS' PRACTICAL SERVICE PROJECTS

One highlight of that last year with my class that completed Standard VI in 1973, was the two weeks of practical service that the students and I gave to help the pastors and Christians in some of our outstations. Together we helped put a new grass roof on a church at the *Opiyepulu* Outstation. Then at the *Akepangi* Outstation we repaired a fence around a garden for a lady, and also gave first aid to children afflicted with scabies and other minor sores. It was at the *Kelge* Outstation, however, that we stayed a whole week, living as a group of 12 of us in the pastor's small bush house. He and his family had moved into the house *where the pigs were kept,* so we could use their house during this time! (Can you imagine that?)

Joy and I used sleeping bags, but the boys just had blankets to sleep on the grass floors around the open fire-pit in the middle of the room. The first night there, during the night I began to feel unusual warmth in my feet, only to discover that my feet (in the sleeping bag) were nestled on the warm ashes in the fire-pit! With that, I quickly realized I needed to change my sleeping position! In the other small room of the house the girls were safely bedded down with their blankets—away from a similar possibility.

At this outstation we visited the different homes of the area, giving encouragement and help in whatever way was needed. I even ended up giving one of my dresses to a lady who had none at all. She was so happy, and wore it continuously after that! We also had lots of fun playing outdoor games together while there, and even enjoyed the *strenuous* trek up the side of the mountain (with all our baggage) to get to where the outstation was located. The journey back down the mountainside was much easier, however, and we were glad!

During those two weeks the students were graded for their show of cooperation and willingness to work without complaining, for their proper Christian attitudes toward one another, and for their overall teamwork ethics. They were also rewarded with an allowance to help them with their next year's school fee. Many of them were planning to continue with Grade 7 at the *New Guinea Bible Institute*—the new school located at the *Pabarabuk Station.*

(All these students had already taken the same exam as was given at accredited schools for entrance into high school, yet even those who *might pass* the exam would not be eligible to go to high school since our Bible Center was not an accredited school. Likewise, even some students at accredited schools who *did pass* the exam could not enter high school either—just because there just wasn't enough room in the high schools for all who were eligible! That meant that all throughout the country, at the end of each school year there would be many *school-leavers* [as they were called] who were unable to continue their education. As a result, *rascal activity* was beginning to increase rapidly throughout the country. [As the years passed, this activity included gang rape, theft, property destruction, and all sorts of crimes.] So...that is why the new school at Pabarabuk was being opened up—to help give opportunity for many of these *Grade 6 school-leavers* to continue their education and graduate after completing Grade 10, as they do in the government high schools.)

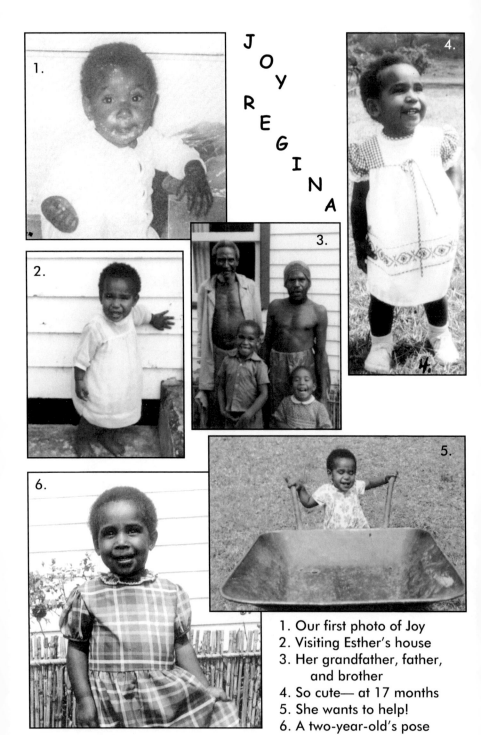

JOY REGINA

1. Our first photo of Joy
2. Visiting Esther's house
3. Her grandfather, father, and brother
4. So cute— at 17 months
5. She wants to help!
6. A two-year-old's pose

66

Chapter 6

FRIGHTENING EXPERIENCES

I would also love to mention the names of *all* the students I taught at Tambul, telling you interesting stories about different ones, but there are too many. However, *Namba* (the Pidgin word for *number*) is one I cannot avoid mentioning by name. He experienced a near-death incident when he was my student at Tambul —possibly 12-14 years of age at the time. Here is a story about him.

Namba spent a lot of time with Daniel and learned quickly about the work in the fields with the tractor and other equipment. As a result, Daniel taught him to drive the tractor and help with some of that kind of work. One day, however, a very tragic accident occurred when Daniel was working in the field. He was trying to prepare a path at the top of a ridge for the cattle to go down to the river below, when his tractor started sliding off the side of the ridge. At that time, he called for Namba to help him by using a second tractor to pull him back on track again. Namba had observed at other times when Daniel was pulling something hard or heavy with the tractor, that the front wheels of the tractor would sometimes lift up off the ground, but he also observed that the wheels would always come back down to the ground again. So, when he was pulling Daniel's tractor that day, and the front wheels lifted off of the ground, he did not realize that for them to come back to the ground *he had to push in the clutch*. This he did not do! Instead, the tractor kept lifting up higher and higher on its back wheels, and suddenly it flipped over backwards, coming down on top of Namba! When Daniel saw what had happened, he was *horrified*—thinking that *surely Namba was killed by the impact!* Frantically, with the help of a couple garden workers, Daniel and the others were miraculously able to lift the tractor off of Namba, only to find that he had not even lost consciousness! His head, however, was split open across the top of his forehead, and back over his head a short way, revealing what looked like brain matter. He was rushed to the nearby government clinic, but they could not deal with such an injury there. They only bandaged his head, and from there he had to be taken *on the back of the truck* to the Mt. Hagen hospital—three hours away over rough mountainous roads. They also could do little for him there, either, so the next day he was taken by plane to a much larger hospital in *Goroka,* in the *Eastern Highlands.* I spent the night with him at the Mt. Hagen Hospital, as he lay there in the operating room—still fully conscious; but the next morning he was *alone* as he was flown to the Goroka Hospital. Later that day Esther Hershey drove all the way to Goroka to be with him for several days. Otherwise he was all alone—many miles away from his home and people he knew. We had no idea how long he would need to be there.

Of course, in the midst of all this, much fervent prayer was being sent heavenward for him, and God graciously answered! To our great surprise, *one week later* we saw him walking the streets of Mt. Hagen with a big bandage on his head—well on the way to a complete recovery! Under the bandage He had a huge scar across his forehead and on the top right side of his head, but otherwise he looked in perfect health! Oh, how we praised the Lord for His mercy and healing power! *Many important lessons* were learned from that incident!

Namba's testimony shortly after the accident was printed in the 1972 December issue of the *Mission Messenger. Here is what he says:*

MY TESTIMONY

" I am Namba Koe, the boy who had the accident
with the tractor at Tambul. The Lord has healed me,
and now I'm back at Tambul. I'm praising the Lord
because of His wonderful help to me.
When I was under the tractor, I felt that
my angel was there lifting up the tractor, and I didn't feel any
pain. Also, when I was at the Goroka Hospital
I was alone, and trying to think about Tambul,
but something in me told me like this:
'I am with you, Namba. Don't think about your friends.'
When I felt that, I thought, 'My friend is with me,
and that made me very happy.'
This is my little testimony.
Thank you for praying for me."

Namba Koe

Another devastating situation occurred during our 4½ years at the Tambul Station. It took place in 1972 when an extremely dry season came to the Tambul Valley region. Usually we had rain showers every day, along with beautiful sunshine and warm temperatures every day as well. Those showers kept everything plush and green, the sweet-potato and vegetable gardens growing profusely, and our water tanks filled with all the water we needed. However, there were occasionally *dry seasons* when there were not the usual daily rain showers—but such seasons did not usually last long enough to become troublesome. In 1972, however, the dry season stretched out for weeks—and even months; and in addition to that, the temperatures went so low during the clear, moonlit nights until frost killed the sweet-potato (kaukau) gardens all throughout the region. That meant a famine of the people's most important staple food—*kaukau!* Finally, the

Government stepped in and provided bags of rice by the ton, to be distributed to the villages all throughout the area. Our mission station was one of the places where the village people would come to get their portion of rice, and Daniel's job was to help bring the rice from Mt. Hagen and see that it was distributed according to the specifications. Even after the rains came again, and temperatures were back to normal, the Government continued to help the people by bringing in from other areas of lower altitude huge truck loads of kaukau leaves, which were used to start new gardens.

It was also during this time of drought that tribal fighting began to break out in the Tambul Valley. For many years previously, the problem of tribal fighting had been brought under control and was being well maintained by the Australian Kiaps in the area. However, one morning we awoke to see smoke rising from the villages at the far semi-circle end of the valley where two of our outstation churches were located. When the situation was investigated, it was discovered that 40 houses had been burned, trees were cut down, pigs were killed, small village trade stores were damaged, and gardens were destroyed all throughout that area. People were wailing and crying, and many of them—especially women and children—had escaped to other villages for safety. Neighboring village tribesmen were the perpetrators of this destruction, in an attempt to pay back for the *drowning death* of someone from their tribe. The people of this village were blamed for having caused the death by the use of poison. Now, as a result, there was retaliation against those tribesmen, and tribal unrest and fighting continued on—spreading from area to area for years afterwards. At that time however, we missionaries were not endangered by the tribal warfare, even though the people in the villages were experiencing much unrest and fear for their own safety as they moved about in their daily activities—especially in their gardens. In those days, many children were also hindered from attending school as well, and eventually we had to discontinue our classes for the younger children, with only two classes being able to continue and complete Grade VI.

While telling you about our life at Tambul, I must include another incident that highlights the protecting hand of God in our journeys from place to place over the treacherous mountainous roads. On one occasion we were going to a baptismal service at one of our more-distant outstations. We could drive part of the way over the mountain pass, and from there we had to walk the rest of the way over the mountain trail to the outstation. Because many of our students wanted to go with us, we hitched a trailer behind the truck, with some of the students on the truck and some on the trailer. Along the way we met other Christians who were walking to the baptism as well, so we stopped and picked them up, making our load heavier and fuller. Then, suddenly, as we went around one of the sharp turns on the mountain road, the loose gravel on the side of the road caused the trailer to jack-knife with the truck, and having a heavy load on the trailer caused it to flip over on its side—still attached to the truck! Feeling the jolt, I quickly looked back (from inside the truck) and what I saw horrified me!

"Stop, stop!" I screamed, *"Oh! Oh! My children!"* I yelled frantically. *"They're all over the road!"*

Actually, they were mostly scattered *along the side of the road*, and not all over the road! Immediately we stopped and got out of the truck in a jiffy; I began going from child to child to see who, and how badly, each one was hurt. I can't remember all the details, but some of them were not hurt at all—only terribly frightened. Of the others, however, one was bleeding from a cut at the ear, another had a dislocated wrist, and still others had minor injuries which my memory now fails to recall clearly enough to describe. Two or three who were more seriously injured were taken to the hospital clinic in Mt. Hagen—which was still quite a distance away—and three or four others were treated at a small clinic in a nearby village. The rest of the passengers walked the rest of the way to the baptism. Then, when things were under control again, we followed after them! Oh, how we thanked the Lord that there were no *more-serious* injuries, and that, except for a few remaining scars, those who had been injured recovered quickly. Once again, this experience was one from which we learned important lessons—both about being more responsible for the safety of our children, and also about God's loving hand of protection and care even in the midst of what *could have been a fatal tragedy!* God is *SO* faithful, and even now I praise Him for His goodness and mercy during those days! Truly we were humbled and realized more than ever our total dependence on God's love and care for us and for our people.

SAVED by a ROCK

and

RESCUED by a LOADED BEER TRUCK

This miraculous incident occurred on the occasion when it became my lot to bring home from Mt. Hagen a small Land Rover vehicle which so happened to be badly in need of repairs. (It had only two doors, one of which did not operate properly—on the driver's side—and besides that, only the front brakes were working; also, it would not start without being pushed or pulled.) Since this was an emergency situation, and since the vehicle was in town and had to be taken home, it was also loaded with a supply of rice that was needed at the Tambul Station. I can not recall all the details, but for some reason I was in town and was given the task of driving the vehicle home—a three-hour trip across the mountains to the Tambul Station.

After someone in town helped me get the Rover started, I was on my way (alone) with my load of rice bags. All went well during the first part of the journey, until I came to the area where the road had many curves as it wound its way across the mountains.

Taking care not to be going too fast, however, was not quite enough to avoid what happened next. As I was coming upon another sharp curve where there was a lot of loose gravel, I found it necessary to apply the brakes to make the turn. However, with the weight of the rice in the back, and the lack of rear brakes, the Rover simply would not let me complete the turn. Instead, the Rover skidded right into the gravel at the corner—going straight ahead toward the huge rock at the edge of the mountain cliff. *It was the rock that saved me from going over the cliff, and I was so thankful!* However, the impact caused my vehicle to come to a dead stop—engine included! So there I sat, unable to get out of my seat, just thanking the Lord for not letting me plunge down the mountainside! *BUT—what was I to do now? The only thing I could do was to pray—so that's what I did!*

In my prayer I told the Lord that I needed someone to come along and help me get my vehicle started again, so I could get on the rest of the way home. Then I sat and waited! After waiting patiently for a period of time, I finally heard the sound of a truck coming. And would you believe it! It was none other than a big truck loaded with a supply of *BEER!* Of course the truck stopped, and the driver offered to give me help—which he did. He used his truck to give me the help I needed to get the Rover started again, and then also helped me get back on the road headed in the right direction toward home. I chided the driver a bit for the kind of load he was carrying, but I truly thanked him for his kindness in giving me the help I needed. Just having a *loaded* truck come along at just the right time was indeed an answer to prayer—regardless of the kind of load it was carrying!

Again, much more could be included about our life at Tambul. To say the least, I must admit that our busy schedules of teaching children and pastors, farm management, parenting, making weekly treks to outstations up and down dangerous mountainous trails and preaching in outstations, assisting with large baptisms at numerous outstations, being host & hostess (along with the help of the other missionaries on our station) for large gatherings of missionaries and church leaders from other EBM stations, building new buildings, and even making preparation for opening a *Pidgin Bible School*—all this took its toll on our young lives. Nevertheless, by God's help and *a few* brief times of much-needed refreshment, we completed 4½ years at Tambul. Then we were asked to move to the new, recently acquired *Pabarabuk Station* where the *New Guinea Bible Institute* had been already in progress for two years.

ABOVE:
The Outstation Pastors Daniel taught each week

LEFT:
Daniel, Esther Hershey, Joy and I (on a sunny day)

Chapter 7

A NEW SCHOOL at TAMBUL

~~PIDGIN BIBLE SCHOOL~~

When *New Guinea Bible Institute* opened in 1972, that same year a new *Pidgin Bible School* was scheduled to be opened at Tambul as well. Prior to that time, much planning was going into opening the Bible Institute at Pabarabuk, and several new missionary families were going to live at that station to help with the new school. I was somewhat puzzled about the fact that nothing was being said about the proposed new school at Tambul. Therefore, at one of our business meetings, I recall asking, *"Who will be coming to Tambul to help with the opening of the Pidgin Bible School?"*

I can't recall who answered me, but the answer was simply, *"You're there!"*

So—what did that mean for me? I soon realized that it simply meant that *in addition to* the Bible Center (which by then numbered more than 100 students), the new *Pidgin Bible School* was to be opened that year also—and that meant that much more work had to be done before we would be ready for the new school year to start in 1972!

Not being an experienced organizer—especially for a Bible School—(which I never attended myself), *I had to definitely have God's help for this specific job.* There were schedules to be planned, integrating times for classes and work periods for the Bible School students—all blending in with the Bible Center schedule already in progress on the station. There needed to be research as to what subjects were to be included, and assignments given as to who would be available to teach each class, dividing the work load between the three teachers who would be coming to teach in the school. Though I would not personally be teaching any of the Bible classes, there were also classes for music and health for which I would need to be responsible—if they were to be taught at all. It was all so new and foreign to me to make all these plans, but by the time the new school year began, the Bible School was opened with both teachers and students ready to begin as scheduled. All I can say is, *"The LORD was my helper!" Only by His help* had I been able to complete what was expected of me to do! (Details concerning housing and food supply for the new staff and students were not mine to arrange, for Daniel and his station helpers had taken care of that part.)

As for a music class, that became a most enjoyable class for all of us—both the Bible Center and Pidgin Bible School as well. Using my accordion as a helper, we learned many songs that were new to them and a blessing to all of us. Even little Joy learned to sing *"He Touched Me,"* (both in English and Pidgin) by the time she was four years old. She learned it just by hearing the students singing in music class and chapel times.

With the *two* schools now completing their second year together on the station, 1973 was coming to a close and it was time for us to have a furlough—the first since August of 1969! At the beginning of that year we had also begun to seek information from the Welfare Department about having the proper permission to take Joy home with us on our furlough. It was the Welfare Agent herself who asked if we would like to *adopt* Joy, for we had no idea at that time that such an arrangement might be possible. We then agreed that we would be so happy if it could be done. With that, the agent began the legal process that took almost the full year to get the final approval, making her legally our very own—*Joy Regina Glick!* The letter stating the completion of the process was received in December, telling us that they wanted to complete it in time to be our 1973 Christmas gift! We were *so happy* when that letter of good news reached us!

(As things turned out, however, we did **not** go home for a furlough at the end of 1973 after all!)

During that year, final arrangements were finally being made to bring to Tambul another missionary couple—*Bob and Barb Brock.* Bob was a Bible School graduate who would be the new, official *Director* of the *Tambul Bible School.* Personally, I had been praying and requesting such a change for the good of the school for quite a long time, for I felt the school needed more experienced oversight and direction than what I was able to provide. However, this change of station personnel meant that we would also be making *a change of location*—instead of going home for a furlough! The furlough would have to be delayed. As the Brocks would be coming to the *Tambul Station,* we would be going to the *Pabarabuk Station*, and the *John Bronniman* family would be moving from Pabarabuk to the *Pulupatu Station* where the Brocks were presently stationed. God had so blessed and helped Daniel with the management of the Tambul Station, so as we were about to leave the station, it was financially in good order. Now he was needed at Pabarabuk to help do the same kind of management there. As for me, it was also planned that I would continue with teaching duties at the Bible Institute in 1974. This made me very happy, for it would also mean that I would also be continuing to teach most of the students who had completed Standard (Grade) 6, with me as their teacher all the years since 1969.

As you might expect, leaving Tambul was a very sad occasion for all of us—our pastors, the station workers, the staff and students of both schools, our one fellow-missionary on the station, Esther Hershey, and Kinie—our faithful house-girl. We would even miss our treks to many of the 18 outstations we had visited numerous times, as well as the Christians there. On our last Sunday at Tambul, hundreds of Christians from the village outstation churches walked many miles to come for a *"bung"* service in the tabernacle on the mission station. Afterwards there was much show of affection between us and them, with many tears and warm embraces. Nevertheless, by then God had also prepared our hearts and minds to willingly move on to the next assignment He was giving us, and we did so with peace and anticipation.

Part of a "bung" crowd of worshippers gathered inside the Tambul Station's large Tabernacle. The people have come from many of the Outstation Churches that were within walking distance. Note the two classrooms near the entrance of the tabernacle— one with the blackboard lifted up for people to be seated there as well.

Chapter 8

PABARABUK STATION
and
NEW GUINEA BIBLE INSTITUTE

Our move to Pabarabuk was exciting, and again full of new challenges. The house where we would be living was built by John Bronniman, but it was not completely finished yet. It was a large, black-shingled house, and very interesting—with an open stairway leading to three rooms on a second floor built over the back half of the house. The bathroom, one bedroom, and a small office were on the main floor in addition to space for cooking, dining, and living, and even a fireplace! Between the bedroom and the office, a foyer-like area had a door leading to a patio and the yard behind the house.

When we first moved in, we had a problem with fleas in the one upstairs room that we were not planning to use—except when we had company. We didn't know where the fleas came from, but they were jumping all over the place! Getting rid of them was quite a challenge! Finally, however, after doing everything we could imagine to do, the fleas were completely cleared out, making the room usable for any purpose! What a relief!

On one occasion, however, when two of Daniel's brothers and their spouses had come to visit us, one of the couples found a *dead rat* under their bed! I was really aghast—and truly humiliated! Sometime earlier we had detected a bad odor in the house, but we thought we had gotten rid of the odor and its source after discovering the tail of a rat hanging through a crack between the boards in the ceiling of our bedroom on the first floor. Because we had already gotten rid of that critter—and the sickening odor—we were so surprised at what was found in the guest room! Nevertheless, we embarrassingly apologized for the presence of that *unwelcome, smelly, occupant* under the bed, and quickly got it out of the way—doing our best to immediately refresh the room for our guests to re-occupy with comfort. All in all, we enjoyed living there because it was nice and roomy; there was plenty of space for many guests, and we had a lovely, productive family garden beside the house.

This house, however, was located near the entrance of the station—before going down the hill into a ravine, across a bridge, and up the next hill to the other side where the main station was located—with an airstrip down the middle of it. That is where my classroom was—down toward the far end of the airstrip. Early each morning I had a long walk to my classroom for my prayer-time in my little classroom office. Then Daniel bought himself a *little* Honda motorcycle to move around more quickly on the station to do his work, so I also used it for my early morning trips to the classroom! That was a blessing and time-saver for me!

Later, when *Dean* and *Brenda Rose*, with their family of four young boys, came to live at Pabarabuk, they needed a large house. Daniel was then appointed to build another house for us—a little bungalow—and the Rose family lived in the large, black house. We also liked living in our new bungalow very much. It was much closer to the classroom where I taught, and there we also had a big, productive *pineapple* garden just behind the house. A cluster of *banana* trees and some *papaw (papaya) trees* grew right in our yard, and a vegetable garden was at one end of the yard as well. These gardens and trees provided good, healthy eating for us, with enough to share with other missionaries and students living on the station as well!

By this time the Bible Institute had grown to 120 students for the 1974 school year. There would be *Year 1, 2, and 3* students—that is, Grades 7, 8, and 9. The first two years of the school had been conducted with the teachers being monitors for the students as they were doing correspondence studies provided by the Government. As a result, some of the students from the first class were already able to move on to the *Nazarene School of Nursing* or to one of the available *Teachers' Colleges* for further training when they had finished Grade 8. By1974, however, some of the correspondence lessons were no longer being provided for the students, so teachers would have to provide their own materials for those subjects. Because I would be teaching the English classes, I still had access to the special English correspondence lessons for that year. That was truly a blessing for me, for those lessons were *very different* compared to the English lessons I had taught at our church school in Ohio. (Remember—English for these students was a *foreign language*, and not the language they speak at home with their families.)

In addition to two *English* classes, I had a *Music* class with all 120 students, and also a large *science* class—using books that had been donated to us from USA. Other missionary teachers taught Bible, math, social studies, history, sewing, typing, health, carpentry, mechanics, gardening, etc. During our later years there, *Bible*, *child evangelism*, *bookkeeping*, and being *accompanist* for the choir were also classes on my teaching list. And in addition, one year I also gave *piano lessons* to a small class of students and helped with a *typing* class as well.

Eventually, teaching music was finally passed on to other more-qualified teachers who had become available. (Nevertheless, when no one else was there to do a certain task, or to teach a certain class, it was my *privilege* to pick up the slack and give of my best in doing what other *trained* personnel could do much better—until they were available to do so. This is a lesson I learned very quickly in all our time in New Guinea, and I found it very amazing how *often* God had given me the wisdom and ability I needed for specific tasks when I sought His guidance and help, and then did my best with what He had given me!)

After being at Pabarabuk for one year, it was definitely time for us to take our furlough—5½ years from the time we left home! This we did, leaving in December of 1974, and returning back to New Guinea six months later, in 1975. We enjoyed that time at home—especially having Joy (then 4 years old) with us. She was a delight to all the family and everywhere we went to share news of God's work in New Guinea. She would always sing her song, *"He Touched Me"*—sometimes in both English and Pidgin, which delighted the hearers. She was truly a blessing to us! At the age of four she was able to speak both English and Pidgin quite fluently—for a child her age.

PAPUA NEW GUINEA—AN INDEPENDENT COUNTRY

The furlough was quite refreshing for both Daniel and me, but for me, especially. When the six months were up, I was quite eager to get back to my work in the classroom once again by mid-1975. Then, later on that same year, some big changes took place in the country: New Guinea became *'Papua New Guinea'* and the New Guinea Bible Institute became *'Papua New Guinea Bible Institute.'* You see, that is when the southern half of the country—known as *Papua,* and the northern half—known as *New Guinea,* were joined together to be <u>one Independent Country</u> under a *Central Government* in the *Capital City* of *Port Moresby.*

For money, we had used English *pounds and shillings*—when we first went there. Later that was changed to Australian *dollars and cents,* but at this time the name of their *new* money became *KINAS and TOEAS.* (Kina is the name of a valuable shell used in tribal bridal- pay exchanges. I'm not sure about the name *toea,* but possibly it is also a kind of shell.)

It may greatly interest you to know that it is clearly stated in Papua New Guinea's Constitution that Papua New Guinea is a *Christian* Country! It was through the influential lives and work of many missionaries over a period of years, that this new, independent country had chosen to give honor to God in this way.

The opening of the *Central* government under the leadership of a *Prime Minister* was soon followed later by the opening of *Provincial* governments with their own *Ministers* to be representatives in the Central government. It was a wonderful privilege for our *PNGBI Choir* to be invited to sing some national and Christian songs at the opening ceremony in *Mt. Hagen*—the *Provincial Capital* of the *Western Highlands Province. Joanna Wehrman* was the choir director at that time, and it was my privilege to work along with her with the musical accompaniment. On the following page are the words of one of the songs the choir sang. It is sung to the tune of *"Home on the Range,"* using words the Lord inspired me to write for the occasion.

Opening day for the Western Highlands Provincial
Government Center—in white: PNGBI Choir singing.

**SONG SUNG by the PNGBI CHOIR
at MT, HAGEN. W.H.P.
for the
OFFICIAL OPENING
of the
WESTERN HIGHLANDS PROVINCIAL GOVERNMENT,
1975**
(Choir Director: Joanna Wehrman)

OUR HOME—PAPUA NEW GUINEA
(Tune: Home on the Range)
-1-
This beautiful land, PAPUA NEW GUINEA,
where rivers and mountains abound;
Where gardens produce plenty food for our needs,
and flowers shed beauty around.
-Chorus-
HOME, our beautiful home,
this land of PAPUA NEW GUINEA;
Thank GOD for our land, so great and so grand,
our HOME, so happy and free.
-2-
We remember to pray for our leaders each day,
That God will direct all their ways;
For the freedom we enjoy, through the leaders we have,
To GOD be all glory and praise!
-Chorus-
Praise be to our GOD,
our thanks to the LORD we proclaim,
For our country so free. Where we have liberty,
To worship and honor HIS NAME!
To worship and honor HIS NAME!
To worship and honor HIS NAME!

ABOVE:
The attractive entrance to the main campus of the Papua New Guinea Bible Institute. This area later became the burial place for two of our EBM missionaries.

ABOVE & RIGHT:
2 students display some fresh bananas from the trees in our yard, and delicious vine-ripened pineapples from our pineapple garden behind the house.

BRIEF HISTORY of the PABARABUK STATION

Being one of the earliest stations under the work that was started in 1948 by EBM's pioneer missionary, *G.T. Bustin,* his partners, and his family, it was later carried on under the leadership of Australian missionaries. Then in 1972, it was again brought back under the leadership of Evangelical Bible Mission, and that is when the New Guinea Bible Institute was opened under the effectual leadership of *Winston Wehrman.* It was Winston's vision to minister to the many school-leavers throughout the country by providing for them an opportunity to continue their education through Grade 10 and to know the *Gospel of the Lord Jesus Christ* through the teaching of God's Word. God greatly blessed him in this endeavor, in cooperation with EBM, making this vision truly become a reality. As a result, the students that attended school there came from all parts of the country of Papua New Guinea, and from numerous mission backgrounds. Today they have spread all throughout the region—even beyond the nation of PNG, carrying the message and influence of the Gospel of Jesus Christ wherever they have gone. Though many students may not have remained faithful, the seed of God's Word has been planted in their hearts and lives, and His Word will not *"return void."* (Read Isaiah 55:6-11.)

Located among the mountains of the Western Highlands—not far from the *Southern Highlands Province* where the *Kauapena Station* is located, the school sits on the two sides of a large, previously-used airstrip. Many buildings were added along this airstrip as the station developed: missionary and national staff housing, student dormitories and classrooms, a large chapel and classroom complex, an administration building, the student kitchen and dining hall, a mechanic shop, a carpenter shop, a library, sewing room and printing room complex—all helping to fill the space next to the airstrip. At the one end of the airstrip, a guest house was also built, as well as a new clinic building—near the location of the local church. Beautiful hedges of poinsettia bushes adorned the sides of the airstrip, with other large flowering trees and frangipani adding their beauty as well.

The local village of *Pabarabuk* and a small schoolhouse for local *primary* students are located just behind the mission buildings on the right side of the airstrip. In addition, the station has much garden space for growing lots of kaukau (sweet potatoes) and all kinds of vegetables. There is also a pineapple garden and some banana and papaw trees—for students and staff, as well as many acres of coffee trees to be harvested, processed, and marketed. The area across the river (called *Bilico*) is used for cattle or more gardens, and there is also a piggery for raising pigs. Located near the entrance of the station is a trade store to provide staple goods for the local village and the school. In total, the *Pabarabuk Station* became a central meeting-place for nationals and missionaries of all EBM stations in New Guinea for conferences and camp meetings.

I am telling you all these details so that you can visualize at least a little the outstanding situation, location, and importance of the Bible Institute at Pabarabuk. I also want you to rejoice with us for all that the Lord has been doing in PNG through the work and ministry of the many *EBM* missionaries and national workers associated with *Evangelical Bible Mission,* who have had a part in the ministry activities at *this place*, (as well as at schools on other *EBM* stations.) From these sources have come national missionaries, pastors, and evangelists—all helping to spread the Gospel of Jesus Christ in all parts of the country. Likewise, there are also political leaders, ambassadors, doctors, nurses, bankers, businessmen, carpenters, mechanics, educators, musicians, and all sorts of Christian laymen who are living and working for the Lord to this present day, who were once a part of the schools provided by *EBM*. To GOD be all the glory for the work of *the Kingdom of God* being done there!

LARGE TASKS—LITTLE MISSIONARIES
BIG GOD!

As you have already seen, both Daniel and I have been very active in ways we were never *educationally* trained to function. But here again I want to give praise to the Lord for the way He has led and directed our lives simply through our yielding to *Him* in regards to the choices we have made, and letting ourselves be available where there were specific needs. *To Him be all the praise for the accomplishment of each task given to us along the way.*

One task that was passed on to Daniel, which affected my schedule as well, is that of *Field Leadership* of the *EBM* work in *New Guinea*. From the beginning, when this assignment was given to Daniel in 1972 (while we were still living at Tambul) it seemed to be something much bigger than his ability and qualifications. However, when *Gerald Bustin*, (the Field Leader at that time), had to leave the country unexpectedly because his wife *Roana* had been stricken with hepatitis and could not recover adequately, he asked Daniel to *temporarily* fill this position for him. Later, at the next *EBM Board meeting* in USA, he was given this task *officially*. While the task was a big responsibility, he submitted to it as requested, depending on the help of the *LORD* to carry it out—and with my help as his secretary!

Being the *Field Leader* meant that Daniel needed to be aware of the work, activities, and needs of each of the seven main stations. This we did together, making visits to each one periodically. Daniel's main giftedness for this task was his ability to manage finances well and give guidance along those lines. My part was to collect financial status reports from each station in order to provide information for the reports required by the Government. Then quarterly financial reports were also sent to the EBM Board at home as well, all a part of my secretarial duty.

Now that we were at Pabarabuk, Daniel carried on the responsibility of station management just as he had done at Tambul, along with the Field Leader's duties. So here again, the secretarial work and financial records continued to be my part—by virtue of my being his wife! (I didn't really mind, though, for I always liked that kind of work—right from the beginning of our marriage, and long before I began teaching.) Later however, when my load was getting too heavy, I taught one of my bookkeeping students, *Nelson Wahune,* how to help me keep the station's financial records, and that was a blessing. He did an excellent job—both in neatness and accuracy. (After graduating at PNGBI, Nelson worked in a bank and was able to rise to a high level position at the bank where he worked.) Another local student, Jack Kawa, also helped with this work for a time. He did a very good job as well. I was very pleased with their academic and practical performance, and even more so, I was so thankful that they had both responded positively to the message of the Gospel as well.

PNG BIBLE CHURCH

In 1975, during our first year at Pabarabuk, a very outstanding *milestone* was reached in the ministry of the Evangelical Bible Mission in Papua New Guinea—namely, the organization of the *PNG Bible Church.* I recall when we lived in the big black house across the ravine from the airstrip, that our house was a meeting place for the missionary station-managers, and the national head-pastors and church leaders from each of the seven main stations. These meetings were long discussion and planning sessions for sharing the missionary-leadership positions with our national brothers and forming what would be called the *PNG Bible Church.* When final decisions were made, everything had to be written down, translated into Pidgin, and put into print. My part in the whole process was to help with getting these jobs done. It may be interesting to you to know that out of those times of prayer, deliberation, decisions, and final conclusions has come a church body in Papua New Guinea that has grown to include the statistics as of May 2007 which you can read in the Appendix at the end of this book. You will be amazed at what God has been doing through the years since the days our time in PNG ended in 1987. (See page 167.)

A VERY BUSY YEAR!

So much more could be told about our years at Pabarabuk, but I cannot fail to tell you of the two most outstanding years of all the rest. First, in 1976, I experienced what I would call the *busiest* year of my life. Nevertheless, it was also one of the most *enjoyable* years of my teaching years at Pabarabuk. Besides teaching my usual classes, taking care of the secretarial duties for Daniel as EBM's Field Leader, and being responsible for the financial records of the school and station, I had to fill in for two of our staff who would be home for furlough that year. For *Esther Hershey,* I had to take over her English II class, in addition to my own.

It was during that second full year of teaching there, that I had to provide all the English materials I needed for as many as 60 students. Using another student's completed correspondence lessons to copy from, we typed all those lessons on stencils and made copies from them on an old mimeograph machine. Then we assembled the pages together into covered booklets for distribution to my students. A new set of two booklets (20-40 pages each) had to be ready for each student at the beginning of each of the three terms of the school year. To accomplish this, God provided me with some very good student helpers—Milo Timini and Pelae. Oh, how I needed them, and what a blessing they were to me! I soon learned that the Lord always provides *just what we need at the right time* when we take Him at His Word and fully trust in Him! (When Esther Hershey was available, we all worked together at the task, but we missed her help when she was on furlough.)

Marie Trapani had been the *Registrar* for the school up to that year, but her going on furlough left the Registrar's job up to me as well. I cannot describe in a few words what all that job includes, but in brief, it meant that I had to read and respond to nearly a thousand applications, eventually deciding who would be the 200 accepted to come as new students to PNGBI the next year. And finally, since 1976 was going to be the first class to graduate from PNGBI, we wanted to have a yearbook to celebrate the occasion. If it was to be done, I would have to take on the responsibility of planning and helping with that, too. Of course, in all these things, there were numerous student helpers, and a few missionary staff helpers, as well. A volunteer cameraman from another mission also came to help with the yearbook photography. But to say the least, my days that year began very early, and my nights were very short! I often stayed in my classroom office until very late at night, and on several occasions I even stayed there *all night,* sleeping on two wooden folding chairs with very little comfort or sleep throughout the night!

At the house, two of my precious students, *Tame* and *Wandeya Goraiye,* helped prepare meals and look after Joy in the afternoons when she was not in school, and in the evenings Daniel would be there at the house as well. These two girls came from Tambul and were among my original students from 1969. They were sisters, attending the Bible Institute, but they lived part of the time at our house instead of in the Girls' Dormitory. They took turns helping with breakfast and the evening meal so that each of them could also spend time with the other students at mealtimes in the student dining hall. They were truly a blessing to me!

As you're reading this, perhaps you're thinking, *"Where was your good sense?"* And as I look back now, I realize I did not seem to use good sense—trying to keep all those things under control day after day. But at that time I was seemingly energized by the sheer joy of doing what *someone* needed to be doing, and because it fell my lot to do them—I really had no choice! I was busy doing it all for *JESUS*, and I was happy! One thing, however, that helped tremendously to keep things organized for me was the fact that I had a whole 20' x 40' un-needed classroom to work in. With room enough for long tables on which to do the typing and mimeographing, and to spread out the work of correlating the English materials we were producing, plus extra space for the student helpers who corrected students' English workbooks for me, and assembling the materials for the yearbook, etc., the large room was a tremendous blessing. As for the Registrar's work, that was done in the small office adjacent to the classroom, completely separate from the other jobs. Also, the financial record keeping for the station was done in our little office at the house. Sometimes I felt like I was being neglectful of some of the jobs that needed to be done, but in sharing that concern with someone (I cannot remember who), that person gave me a word of encouragement by saying, *"No, you are not neglecting, you are just <u>prioritizing</u> your jobs by doing what needs to be done <u>first</u>."* Wow! That truly was encouraging to me, and I also learned a new word—*prioritizing!* I had never used that word before! In the end, everything got done at the right time—and again, *only by the help of the Lord and the faithful helpers He gave to assist me!* How wonderful!

The large Chapel and 2 classrooms at the PNG Bible Institute

ABOVE: The graduating class of 1978 — the smallest of four classes I helped to teach that year

LEFT: With Milo, my helper in making the books I needed for my English classes

93

EXCITING VISITORS!

That busy year ended by December of 1976. Then came January of 1977 when something entirely different energized me and gave me great excitement! What was so exciting???? Well, just this—my parents—*(Paul & Rhoda Wengert),* Daniel's brother and wife—*(Jacob & Dorothy Glick),* our nephew, his wife, and daughter—*(Lane, Lorena, & Jennifer Glick),* were all coming to PNG to visit us! *Hoorah! Hoorah!* (*Clara Doubledee* also traveled to PNG with them, but she spent her time visiting other missionaries.) Although I still had some registrar's work to complete in the office at the school, for the most part I could spend most all of my time with our family all during the month of January!

During that month, when the school was closed for the end-of-the-year break, Wandeya and Tame were still there with us, so there was a total of 12 of us staying at our house when our visitors were there. We had so much fun together! When we took our visitors to visit some outstations, we all piled into our Toyota Land Cruiser, taking whatever luggage we needed to take with us on top of the vehicle. On our way to the town of *Mendi,* we had two flat tires and had to wait for several hours along the *Highlands Highway* before the tires were repaired and we were again able to proceed on our journey. During that time, Wandeya and Tame sat on the road pavement and played a game of "jacks," using stones as their jacks and ball for their game! That was an interesting innovation for our visitors to observe! Then, as we continued from Mendi to the *Tongo River Outstation,* some of the roads we traveled were so bumpy that Mother's purse bounced right off her lap (where she sat in the front seat) and right out the open window! Of course, we stopped to pick it up, but we had a big, jolly laugh about it. Also, while at Tongo River, Mother took an afternoon rest in one of the bedrooms at Dean and Brenda Rose's house. When she was getting up from her rest, her foot went through the floor near the edge of the bed—all the way up to her knee! There she sat on the floor, laughing and calling out for help to get herself up and out of the hole in the floor! Thankfully, she was not hurt badly by the fall. That too, was quite a funny situation!

We also visited the *Kauapena Station* where the *Wehrmans* had lived before the PNG Bible Institute was started at Pabarabuk. At the time of our visit, however, only *Beverly Wickham,* the missionary nurse, was there to greet us. *Lenita Bustin*, who had been there for many years as well, was on leave at that time. (Joanna and Lenita are sisters of Gerald and Paul Bustin, mentioned earlier in my story. It was their father who had first pioneered the work in the Highlands of New Guinea in 1948.)

We then took our visitors to see the *Tambul Station*—bringing back to us the warm memories of the years we lived there. While there we visited the Brock family and other station workers and teachers who were faithfully working with the Tambul Bible School. These visits were all very interesting to our visitors. However, we did not go to *Pulupatu Station* to visit the *Bronniman family*, or to *Mele Stations* to visit the *Rich family,* for traveling to both of these stations would have taken us over *very difficult roads—even for us missionaries,* let alone visitors! In those days, not only were roads quite treacherous—having lots of rocks and mud to contend with—but most of the bridges were in such a condition that it caused *me* to pray for protection every time we crossed them! Some bridges were simply rough boards laid across huge logs that spanned the gorge with a swift-flowing river below. The construction of bridges is hard to describe clearly, but to the traveler unaccustomed to such conditions, they were not considered to be crossable at all!

(Note the bridge and road photos in the *Appendix.*)

LEFT:
At the airport when our visitors arrived

BELOW:
The bridge to the Pabarabuk Station as it was the day before their departure

ABOVE: Time for haircuts! Lane gets his first

RIGHT: Waiting on the Highlands Highway going to Mendi for the repaired tire after 2 flats

Even the bridge right near our station did not seem crossable to my Dad. The sides of the bridge had been washed out by rains, leaving only a narrow path for a vehicle to cautiously make its way across the waterway below. This condition existed just a few days before it was time for our visitors to leave for home, and Daddy was very nervous about being able to get across that bridge in time for their departure. However, a new, huge drainage pipe was being installed under the bridge for the flow of the water below, so at just the right time the road across the top was restored and their departure was not hindered at all. What a relief that was—especially for Daddy!

(Take another look at the bridge on the cover of this book! That gives you an idea of typical bridges throughout the Highlands at different places—but of course, this particular one was not for vehicles. It is only a foot-bridge! However, we did not cross—or even see this bridge, but some others, like the swinging vine bridges we did cross were scary enough! Another, for instance, was the one with 2 large logs and no planks tying them together. You could walk on only one of them—with both feet—or you could put one foot on each of them. When you would do that, your step would bounce up and down, giving you a terribly shaky, uncertain feeling with each step! I never liked to cross that bridge without holding the hand of someone who was more-experienced at crossing that bridge safely! So be it! Nevertheless, thankfully we always made it safely across!)

One highlight of the time with our visitors was the privilege to attend a baptism at one of the outstations. First we went to the outstation church for a worship service, then together with all the people, we all followed them down the steep mountainside to the place where the mountain stream had been dammed-up, forming a pool where the baptisms would take place. All those being baptized were dressed in long white clothing. How many of them there were at that time, I don't remember now, but likely there were at least 10-20 (or more). Ofttimes there were many more than that at some of the baptisms we attended through the years.

Our visitors also had the privilege of observing some of the activities that take place when there is a death—especially when it is an important person of the tribe. On such occasions, many people are seen along the roads with their bodies covered with mud—including their hair, arms, legs, bodies and faces. This is a usual sign of mourning. The dead body itself is firmly wrapped and hung between two poles, where it is lifted high above the heads of the mourners crowded around below it. There is much loud crying and mourning, which will go on for hours, and even days, before the body is buried. As we were making our trip with our visitors, in one area we came across these activities taking place. It was very interesting to them to actually observe these things in action.

Finally, we were very sad when it was time for our visitors to leave us, but the saddest person of all was *Lorena* (our nephew Lane's wife). She had come on this trip thinking that it was just some exotic experience of excitement and pleasure to visit a tropical land—going half-way around the world; but in learning to know Wandeya and Tame, and meeting many other national Christians, she *fell in love with them and all the people she met!* Also, seeing all the work of the Lord being done there, her heart was gripped with a deep desire to stay there longer and be a part of it all. At the airport her countenance revealed a real sense of sadness because it was time for her to leave these new friends behind.

(As many of you readers may know, however, it was but a couple years later, until Lane and Lorena and their daughter Jennifer returned—not to visit this time, but to work as missionaries. They have an exciting story of their own to tell of their life and work in PNG!)

FOR BETTER or FOR WORSE—LIFE GOES ON!

Even before our visitors left, I had to return to the classroom office to begin welcoming the new students as they were arriving for the new school year. With the Wehrmans home for furlough at that time, a new Principal was taking Winston Wehrman's place. *Glenn Pelfrey* was the one who would fill that position. He and his wife, *Dorothy*, (a nurse) were among the newer missionaries who had come to PNG by this time, as well as the *Gray* and *Antrim families*. Other missionaries—the *Taylors* and *Mrs. Susie Lorimor* (our eldest missionary) had been there since the school opened. Mrs. Lorimor was the teacher for the younger village children who lived next to the Bible Institute, and she was also Joy's teacher when her time came to start school. By now Esther Hershey and Marie Trapani had returned from their furlough and were ready to teach again. So now all these would be part of our missionary staff for the new school year of 1977.

It was exciting to see all the previous students arriving again, and also to meet new students as they arrived. Finally the first day of school began, and things seemed to be moving along very well with all the new staff filling their places. Then one day the bubbles of joy that exuded from my overflowing heart burst into thin air! As a result, instead of beginning another year full of joy and unrestrained energy, from that point on, 1977 became the most disappointing year of my life—thus far!

This was to have been the year my students from Tambul would be graduating—after all the previous years I had taught them—both at Tambul and at the Institute. But now, some of those closest to me as students, (and like children of my own), who were outstanding in their studies and their behavior, were being asked to leave the school! In all, around 70 students left the school—and that took place *right at the very beginning of the school year*! These students would not to be able to return for the rest of the year! My heart was broken! I was so deeply hurt and disappointed, to say the least!

"BUT WHY?"... you may ask. *"What happened?"* The answer may seem simple, but it is also complicated. I cannot explain all the details. To put it briefly, it was because some

well-meaning *would-be-graduating-students* were requesting some changes to be made in regards to the status of the school in relation to the Government. When these changes were denied, some *other under-grad students* unwisely expressed their anger and disapproval by starting a riot! As a result, all those who were *unhappy with the school as it was* were given the opportunity to leave if they did not like the school to remain as it was. But...the *10 leading ones who had suggested the change* (though in a very respectful way) were told to leave—whether they wanted to or not! That is when I lost some of my choice students (and helpers) that would have graduated that year. Truly, I was one bro-ken-hearted teacher, to say the least!

Nevertheless, the school year continued with what was left after the 70 had departed. We still had plenty of students to keep us busy! My energy level, however, was no longer as vibrant and seemingly unlimited as during the previous year, and only by God's help did it turn out to be a good year—in spite of the absence of those choice students weighing heavy on my heart. Otherwise the year was without further incident, and when December came, it was time once again for our furlough. This time, however, it would be for a full year rather than just six months, and emotionally I was truly ready for it!

BLESSINGS and SORROWS of FURLOUGH-TIME

It was so good to be home in USA once again, and to see all our family, relatives, and loved ones there. Daniel's brother Earl and wife Thelma arranged for us to live in their rental house near their home during that year. What a blessing that was! Joy was now eight years old, and it was a good opportunity for her to get better acquainted with her cousins, Barbara and Karen (Earl and Thelma's two daughters) as well as other cousins who lived not far away.

During that 1978 furlough-time, we were again able to attend the yearly camp meeting at the EBM Headquarters in Summerfield, FL. It was there that Joy began her Grade 3 schooling with the *School of Tomorrow, Accelerated Christian Education* studies. The *Sturtevant* family was there at the camp, preparing to go to PNG and start the ACE school for missionary children on the Pabarabuk Station. *Steve and Marilyn* were well-trained for this ministry, and we were so glad Joy would be able to continue her schooling in this way when we would return again to PNG the following year. When we returned to Ohio after the camp meeting, she was then able to do ACE studies at the Peniel Holiness Christian Day School—where for two years I had taught in the high school department of the school many years earlier.

While in Florida at the camp meeting, Daniel and his brother Jim took a two-week trip to Haiti to help a missionary there to build a church. Joy and I would have gone with him, but because Joy could not get a visa, she and I stayed back at the campgrounds until Daniel returned.

During the rest of that year at home we were privileged to make trips to PA to visit my family and relatives several times, but most of the time we were at home in Ohio where Daniel was working at the carpenter trade in order to prepare ourselves financially to return to PNG again. Daniel's brother Jacob had given us a car to use that year, and we were very grateful for that. Then when we were ready to leave again, we were permitted to sell that car to help pay our tickets to go back to PNG. Such trips were very costly, but the Lord always provided what we needed as we did what we could ourselves to live frugally, and as Daniel earned what he could from his work. We also appreciated very much every gift given to us by friends, relatives, or churches—when we were invited to speak of our work in PNG. (However, we did not have any schedule for making deputation visits to numerous churches for this purpose.) Over all, the Lord

Himself was always our sufficient provider! We praise Him for that!

It was in the mid-summer of that year at home that our dear friends, *Sylvanus and Barbara Hostetler*, were called home to meet the Lord through an unbelievable tragic accident! Together they had gone on a motorcycle to visit some friends in Millersburg, OH, As they were returning home, a vehicle collided with them on their cycle, causing the death of both of them. Just two days before, Joy had spent the night at their house while we were speaking at a church in Michigan. (Joy had been scheduled for a dentist appointment in Strasburg during the time we were to be in Michigan, so Barbara offered to let her spend a night with them and take her for her appointment since the dentist was near their home.) Now, just two days after we were at home with Joy again, they were both gone from the scene of life! How unbelievable!!! We were so glad to be home at this time, to help comfort the grieving family at such a time as this. Had it happened while we were in PNG, it would have been even more tragic for us to experience this loss of special friends of ours, with no way to express our sorrow for the pain and loss to their children.

December finally came, and it was time to again head back to PNG. I forget the details of our departure, but usually we spent some time at home with my parents and family in PA around Christmas time when we were home. What we did at this time, and just when we left, I don't recall; but now, for the second time, we were making our departure from the Cleveland, OH, airport. Many local friends, church family, and relatives—as well as Aunts and Uncles from Plain City, OH, and even some of my family from PA, came there to send us off with their love and prayers. It was so heart-warming, yet there were also many tears, for it would be the last we would be seeing each other for another three years.

Local Christians being baptized after the spiritual revival in the Pabarabuk area

The group of students who were baptized after the revival

Wandeya, Joy, & I wash "kaukau" for cooking. Notice the l-o-n-g kaukau in Wandeya's hand.

The Sturtevant family. See story on Page 145.

Tame and Magupia Ugul's wedding. One of the many weddings Daniel performed in PNG. I made all the dresses for this one.

Joy at 8 years of age. Taken during our furlough in 1979.

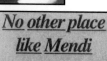

No other place like Mendi

• (right)- A basket weaver, Peter Paima (middle) from Omai village near Mendi and friends display some of his creations
Photo: James Kila

Beautiful baskets and trays can be purchased from these craftsmen.

Chapter 9

SURPRISES – SURPRISES

LAST YEARS at PABARABUK » MENDI » MT HAGEN

It was now 1979, and we were ready for another term of ministry at the Pabarabuk Station. However, as it turned out, we were there only two more years, and then we were asked to move to the *Southern Highlands Provincial Headquarters town of Mendi.* Those last two years of teaching at PNGBI were good years, yet they were different. New missionaries had been added to our missionary family—some at our station, and others where needed at other stations. *Robert and Judy Miller* and family had come to Pabarabuk in 1978, so while we were on furlough, Judy filled my place at the piano—using her *excellent* skill as a pianist. Being a builder, Robert was also able to fill Daniel's place in building while Daniel was missing. During that time he had built a new *Administration Building*, which was a great improvement for the school. Our house became their home while we were gone as well, and we were so glad to have them there—enjoying the pineapples from our garden as well as the bananas and pawpaw from the trees in our yard. However, by the time we got back from our furlough, they had already moved to another station, and our house was ready for us to move back in.

1980 was the last year that *Joanna Wehrman* and I worked together with the PNGBI choir. Joanna was a very excellent director for the choir, being very precise in her ability to hear and produce tones accurately—even without musical accompaniment. My ability as her accompanist was of lesser quality, but I so much enjoyed being permitted to work with her, doing my best at either the piano or accordion. In that year we made two cassette tapes, singing some of our favorites, and even had some of the songs played over the local radio station.

On one occasion our choir was asked to sing at a funeral in the town of Mendi, when a leading government official had been killed in a plane crash. (It was *Paka Kili,* one of our own young men of our mission, who was at that time in a leadership position in the Provincial Government at Mendi, who had asked us to sing.) One song we chose was *"Farther Along, We'll Know All About It,"* which seemed to be very fitting. However, when the Catholic Priest who was officiating in the outdoor ceremony gave announcement of what we would be singing, he announced it this way, *"Father Alone Knows All About It*! That was quite amusing to us! We did not, however, change our words to go along with the title he had announced!

REVIVAL at PABARABUK

Also in 1980, the entire Pabarabuk area experienced a great time of spiritual revival. I cannot recall just how it began, but I know that some of the local Christians were rising very early in the mornings for seasons of prayer. Students and missionaries were also much in prayer, seeking the Lord for spiritual renewal and an awakening among those who were not yet Christians. As the Holy Spirit continued His divine work among us, the students' chapel-times began to turn into times of repentance and making confessions of personal sins and bad attitudes between themselves and other students and teachers. A number of students came to make confessions to me of wrong things they had done in my classes. Daniel also told me that some students had come to him, confessing that they had stolen peanuts, etc. from the gardens. How happy I was to rejoice with them in their new-found forgiveness, peace and salvation through faith in the

Lord Jesus Christ! Many tears of joy were being shed during those days! There was much prayer around the altar, with joyful singing and just a general outpouring of prayer and praise mingled together during meeting times. Not long afterwards many of the students wanted to be baptized, as many of them truly believed and were saved at that time. That was when Joy also, aged 9 years, was among the others who were saved and received water baptism. I forget the exact number, but there must have been around 70 students baptized at that time. In addition, more than 100 new local people were saved, baptized, and added to the *Church* at that time. Even outstations areas were also experiencing the unusual moving and drawing of the Holy Spirit for salvation. How we praised the Lord for the wonderful manifestation of His presence in the school and all the surrounding area during that time of revival. For a long time afterwards early morning prayers were still being heard as people continued to earnestly pray and seek the Lord.

LIFE at MENDI — SOUTHERN HIGHLANDS

The time finally came when we made our move from the busy Pabarabuk Station to the small Mendi Station, located in the outskirts of the small town of Mendi. Here the local language was different from that spoken in Tambul or Pabarabuk, but most of the people could also speak Pidgin. Only the younger people who were privileged to attend school spoke English. Therefore, here we would be communicating more frequently in Pidgin instead of English as we did at Pabarabuk.

Some years before, a work had been started in Mendi town by Gerald Bustin. At that time he was working closely with two young students who were outstanding witnesses for the Lord at the Mendi High School—*Mondopa Mini* and *Wane Ninjipa*. Some time later a church had been built, as well as a house for *Pastor Kalepo Tunge* and his family on the same property. Now, at this time, however, it was planned that Pastor Kalepo and his family would take a break for several months and go back to their home area near the *Mele Station*. While they were gone, Daniel, Joy, and I would live in their house, and Daniel would serve as pastor. (Thankfully, before we had gone home for our furlough, the Field Leadership responsibility had been passed on to another missionary, so that was a *great relief* when we returned to the field again.) Now, filling a pastor's role would be a new challenge for Daniel, but he was happy to have that opportunity—at least temporarily. Also, being relieved of a full-scheduled teaching role when in Mendi would be a welcome change for me. While there, however, I would teach *Religious Instruction* classes in both the Government Primary School and the Government High School. In addition to those classes, I would also teach the children's Sunday School class, and supervise Joy's ACE schooling. All in all, I would be busy enough and be well content with that.

While living in Pastor Kalepo's house, we had a scary experience. One night, when Milo Timini was our guest—sleeping in our extra bedroom, he suddenly awakened when he heard a noise outside. Then he saw a face looking in the window above the café curtain. Quickly he got up, and the face disappeared! He then awakened Daniel and me, and together we went to the kitchen and found the back door slightly open. Everything in sight in the kitchen and living-room seemed to be in place, and we were thankful. We then went outside and found that something to stand on had been placed under Milo's bedroom window, and there were foot-prints on the ground around that area as well. Finally, after investigating around a bit more, and seeing no more clues of missing and disturbed things, we locked the door securely and went back to bed. It was not until in the morning when I went to prepare some eggs for breakfast that I saw that all my eggs were gone from the refrigerator. Then when I wanted to turn on the radio, I discovered the radio/cassette player was also missing! (I was so disappointed about that because one of *my favorite* cassette tapes was in the machine.) I cannot recall clearly, but *I think* there was also a small pan missing from the cupboard. We were amazed at the unusualness of the items that were missing from that theft. *Someone must have been hungry!* Not long afterwards we were informed of some stolen goods at the police headquarters that we could check out to see if any of the things were ours. Sure enough, we were able to recover our radio/cassette player there—but the cassette tape I liked so well was no longer in the machine. *The thief must have liked it too!* We never found out who the thief was, nor the motive for his actions that night.

Since Pastor Kalepo and his family would be returning to pastor the church there again after his break, it became Daniel's job to build another house on the property for us to live in after moving out of Pastor Kalepo's house. The house was built with space under it for the children's class on Sundays, and also space for doing our laundry and for parking our vehicle. Our living quarters were all on one floor above. The outer covering of the house was corrugated iron, and solar panels for heating our water were installed on the roof of the house. What a blessing that was—something we never had before in PNG.

I liked that house very much! It wasn't large, but it was arranged inside to include three bedrooms and an office, in addition to the bathroom, kitchen, and living/dining area. (For a while my Sunday-school class met in the living-room of that house. Later we met in the space under the house.) One leading man of the Mendi area also liked the house so much that he wanted Daniel to build one like it for him. Of course, Daniel could not do it as a money-making project, for his work-permit did not allow him to do business in that way. However, he did build it for him, donating his time, but all the cost of the materials was the man's full responsibility. When it was finished, the man said that when he died, he wanted to be buried in that house!

We very much enjoyed the change of pace and responsibilities at Mendi. This was all *a pleasant surprise* for us, for we did not know what to expect when asked to go there. I also greatly appreciated the privilege of learning to know missionaries from other churches who were living in Mendi, as there were no other EBM missionaries there with whom I could have close fellowship in English rather than in Pidgin. I was then invited to attend the Bible study and prayer-times that a group of these ladies had each week. We ladies represented various mission groups such as the United Church, Pentecost Church, Mission Aviation Fellowship, and PNG Bible Church. (The missionaries from the Baptist Church also became our friends, but the wife did not join us in these meetings.)

LADIES' RETREAT

One day the United Church Bishop's wife, (a lady from Fiji) and another lady from our Bible-study group, came to our house with a request for me. Because they had once heard me speak in Pidgin at a special meeting for ladies there in Mendi, they wondered if I would be willing to be their speaker for their up-coming Ladies' Retreat that they were planning. They needed someone who would be able to speak in Pidgin. The retreat would begin on Friday evening, continue all day on Saturday, and be concluded after the Sunday afternoon session—four sessions in all. On Saturday afternoon there would be some free time, and on Sunday morning the whole church body would be there, so the men would be in charge of that service. The rest of the time would be the speaker's responsibility to fill the session time! *What a SURPRISE that request was for me,* for such speaking occasions were not on my mental list of proposed or probable activities! So then, I told them I had never done something like that before, and I didn't know that I could do it. However, they did not dismiss their request that quickly.

They simply said, *"We believe you can do it, and we will pray for you!"*

How could I resist that kind of encouragement to do even such a new thing? My final answer was, *"I will pray about it, and then I'll do what the Lord tells me to do."*

As I made their request a subject of fervent prayer, the Lord began to give me a subject title and an outline to follow in developing a theme for the occasion. Finally, I told the Bishop's wife that *by God's help and the support of their prayers for me,* I would agree to be their speaker for the retreat. After that, preparations began in earnest for using an overhead projector to visualize for the ladies the messages of each session. I also made booklets that they could fill in blanks from what was displayed on the screen, so in that way they could take the messages home with them. *It was truly the Lord who was my helper* in all this.

Finally, the time for the retreat came, and 103 women came to the United Church in Mendi from all over the Southern Highlands where the United Church had mission outreaches. That Friday evening when the retreat was to begin, I was not feeling well at all! I had a cold, and my head was aching badly. Nevertheless, everything started on time according to the schedule, and by the help of the Lord, I was also in my place. Then, as I began speaking, I felt renewed strength from the Lord as I looked out over that audience of women, and my heart was filled with renewed energy and peace, as the Lord used my lips to speak for Him! At that time also, a persistent thought came to my mind. It was simply this,

"Here I am, speaking to this group of ladies from the United Church, and all our ladies of the PNG Bible Church have never had an opportunity to gather in this way for a retreat—or any kind of special meeting just for them! Couldn't we, of the PNG Bible Church, do the same thing for them?"

(This thought remained in my mind and was given further consideration later—after the retreat was over.)

Well, *by the Lord's help* and the prayers of the ladies, the retreat went very well. So well, in fact, that it was requested that we use the Sunday morning time also—so the men could also hear what the ladies were hearing. *To God be all the praise for the excellent responses of many of the ladies by the time the retreat was finished!* Then, added to that blessing, another request came for me to share at least a portion of the same materials with another group of ladies at the Pentecostal Church—right there in Mendi town. Oh, how our hearts rejoiced for the wonderful privilege to minister to so many in this way!

It was not long after this that the PNG Bible Church (EBM) had its yearly conference when the national church leaders and missionaries from all the church districts and outstations came together at Pabarabuk. It was at that time that I dropped a word to our niece, Lorena Glick (who by then was one of the missionaries at the Kauapena Station), that I thought it would be good for us to have a retreat for our ladies just as the United Church had for their ladies in Mendi. I also told her that since I already had the materials prepared, which I had used in Mendi, I would be willing to give these same lessons and messages for that retreat if we would have one.

Lorena herself, being a gifted leader, took my suggestion to the right place, making a request of the Conference Leaders that we be given approval for having a retreat for the ladies of the PNG Bible Church.

One of the men on the business panel responded in this way—*"What is a ladies' retreat? Would it be for the men, too?"*

"No way!" Lorena answered! *"This would be something special—just for the ladies!"*

Anyway, the end result of that request was that approval was given, and *the very first PNG Bible Church Ladies' Retreat was held in 1982 at the Tambul Station with 92 ladies in attendance! What a wonderful start for a new ministry for these ladies!*

Ladies who attended the Ladies' Retreat at the
Pentecost Church in Mendi

Ladies who attended the first EBM Ladies' Retreat at Tambul

Now, let me interrupt my story here long enough to unveil a scene that took place *25 years after that first retreat.* It was in May of 2007, that Lorena and I traveled again to PNG to attend the celebration of the *25th Anniversary of the Ladies' Retreat.* It was held under a huge tent (used primarily for evangelistic meetings), allowing space for the *thousands* of ladies who filled the tent, sitting on the ground, and filling large areas of the space outside the tent as well. (Note the photo on page 168 of the Appendix.)

I could make a long story about this occasion, but here I only mention that as I viewed the scene of the 5000+ ladies in and around the tent, and later as they lined up in groups for a march through the town of Mt Hagen—all dressed in clothes they had made that represented the Church District they were from, etc., I was overwhelmed by the vastness of the crowd, and the well-planned organization of the retreat as a whole—all done by the ladies of the National PNG Bible Church—without the supervision of missionaries! I was just *overwhelmed with praise to God* for His unspeakable faithfulness to a people who less than 59 years before knew nothing of God the Father, and the Lord Jesus Christ who loves them and gave His life as a perfect sacrifice for their sins, and the Blessed Holy Spirit who gives them power to change their lives from a life-style of head-hunting, tribal wars, polygamy, etc. to lives of righteousness and holiness that honors their Creator! *BLESSED BE THE NAME OF THE LORD!*

◇◇◇◇◇◇◇◇◇◇◇◇◇

It was during the time we were in the Mendi, that prison services in the *Bui Epi Prison* located in that area were begun. One of the men of the Mendi church—*Kapi Kasi*—was a *Warder* at that prison. It was through him that we started going there to share the Gospel of the Lord Jesus Christ with the prisoners—both men and women. Daniel would go with Kapi to speak to the men, giving them a gospel message from the Word, and I would go with his wife to do the same with the women. I would also take along my accordion to provide some music and singing, which the women always enjoyed, along with hearing the gospel lessons given to them. What a challenge it was to minister to prisoners in this way. During that same time *Chuck Colson* had just started the *Prison Fellowship Ministry* in USA—which was also encouraging the prison ministry in PNG as well. (Later on we were privileged to meet Chuck Colson personally at a dinner prepared for him and those involved in prison ministry.)

During our time at Mendi we didn't have many visitors, but it was while we were there that our niece and husband, *LaVina and Samuel McConkey,* came to visit us on their honeymoon. They spent a very brief time there with us, as well as visiting her brother's family—Lane, Lorena, and Jennifer Glick for this special occasion. We were so very happy to have them, and to meet the newest member of our Glick family.

Vacation times for Daniel, Joy, and me were very rare during our years in PNG, but on one occasion while in Mendi, Kapi invited us to go with him and his family to their home village near *Lake Kutubu,* just across the nearby mountains of Southern Highlands. To get there, we flew in a small aircraft to an airstrip near the river leading to beautiful Lake Kutubu. From there we got on a dugout canoe which took us out onto the lake, and then to a landing place along the lake where many, many poorly constructed steps—possibly 50 or more—led us up the mountainside to a house belonging to *Murray Rule, a missionary from Australia*. He and his wife were not in PNG at that time, but it was planned that we would be staying there in their house during our visit. The house and the location was truly interesting, and it was exciting to experience things in this new area of PNG where we had never been before. Kapi and his family left us there at that house and went further on to their own house in the village, but Kapi would be returning later in the day to bring food for us. In the meantime, however, we were already hungry and thirsty! (We should have taken some light food with us, but we had no idea of what to expect, and we had not gone properly prepared with any kind of drink or snack.) When Kapi returned, he brought us some boiled catfish, as well as some sago—both of which we had never eaten before! There was no salt for the fish, and the sago was quite tasteless to us—especially without salt as well! Nevertheless we ate what was served to us, and we survived just fine! (I can't remember what we had to drink.)

(While we were there alone, waiting for Kapi to return, I found a book to read, entitled *"Fasting Can Save Your Life!"* I found it to be quite challenging, especially since it was dealing with *fasting* in relation to health issues and the need for losing excess weight. Some time later I followed its plan and went on a 28 day fast for that purpose. As a result I lost 20 lbs. that I did not regain until more than two years later! I felt so good after those days of fasting!)

The next day Kapi and his sons, John and Henry, and his daughter Goreti, took us on a canoe trip out on Lake Kutubu. They took us along the sides of the lake to show us places where coffins of the dead were put on the rock ledges instead of burying them in the ground. When the bodies in these coffins were fully deteriorated, the bones were taken out of the coffins and placed in lines against the sides of the mountain around the rocky ledges. Skulls were grouped together in one place, while bones from other parts of the body were together in another place. It was quite a gruesome scene to behold! We made stops at two different ledges displaying these kinds of things. In one casket we saw that the body was gone, but the skeleton was still there with pieces of deteriorated cloth draped across the bones. We didn't stay long at these places! It was all so weird, yet it was extremely fascinating to learn about this custom among the tribal peoples of this particular area. They also told us that some bodies were buried in the waters of the lake itself.

ABOVE:
The many
steps to the
house where
we stayed

Scenes along
Lake Kutubu

ABOVE:
and
LEFT:
Bones and
caskets of the
dead along
Lake Kutubu

BELOW:
A group of high
school students who
attended my
Religious Instruction
Class in Mendi

ABOVE:
The house Daniel
built in Mendi

LEFT:
After a Sunday
morning service at
the Mendi Church

RIGHT:
In a village
along Lake
Kutubu

FURLOUGH TIME AGAIN

Before going to Mendi, I was beginning to experience a measure of emotional stress, both from burn-out and from my mid-life crisis-time. At the same time, Joy was also approaching her adolescent years, and between the two, I was not handling things very well—being the supervisor for her ACE studies as well as "Mom." So, after much prayer, we finally decided to let Joy go back to Pabarabuk and attend the *Pabarabuk Area Government Primary School* for a while. While there, she would live in the dormitory with the PNGBI girls. Going to school there, and living with the girls would give her an opportunity to learn to know and understand the ways her own people better—having been raised with Americans in the home—and yet she would be there at the Bible Institute where she could feel at home with other missionaries as well. At that time, Joy seemed quite content and happy with this proposal. So then, from May of 1982 – May, 1983, it was decided for us to take another furlough in the middle of the year, leaving Joy to remain in PNG there at Pabarabuk with the PNGBI girls and the other missionaries until the school year finished in December. At that time she would travel with a *Canadian* missionary family as far as Hawaii, and as the missionary family continued on to Canada from there, she would come the rest of the way alone under the supervision of the Airline Hostess. (This kind of arrangement was entirely new for us, although in those days for many school children in PNG whose parents were from other countries, it was quite common. Joy was 12 years old at that time, so she was still young enough to be under the supervision of the airline staff.) Then, after spending the two months of her school break at home with us in USA, we would send her back to PNG in late January to begin the new school year. That would be really hard for us to do, yet we anticipated joining her in PNG once again after a few more months. Only by God's help did we make it through those days and months of separation. (Looking back, I am not sure that those were the wisest decisions we could have made, but I can only say now that under the circumstances at that time, those were the choices we had made after praying for God's guidance.)

The year at home was a good one, with Daniel having opportunity to work with his brothers at building houses in order to earn what would be needed to pay our fares back to PNG. His brother Earl provided us with a neat, 4th floor apartment to live in during that time. We really appreciated that! In August, we went to the yearly Roxbury Camp Meeting in PA, visiting my family while there, and the following March we also attended the EBM Camp Meeting at Summerfield, FL. Besides that, my brother *Nelson Wengert,* flew his small Cessna to Beach City, OH, bringing his wife, *Jean,* with him to visit us here in OH. That was a wonderful treat for us! In addition to these blessings—having Joy with us for at least two month, and making another visit to PA with my family over Christmas—all these things helped to make the year pass by quickly. I was being refreshed and renewed, and soon we were making our plans to return again to be with Joy and all our beloved people in PNG.

Then, just before we left home to return to PNG at the end of our furlough time, I was informed that when we got back to PNG, I had been appointed to be the *EDITOR* of a new little *news magazine* that Gerald Bustin had envisioned for a long time. Just as EBM's *Mission Messenger* was informing churches, supporters, and friends of the work of Evangelical Bible Mission and all that has been going on under their leadership through the years, this new magazine would be a blessing and service to the PNG Bible Church in PNG in the same way! It was to be published in both English and Pidgin, and would be called the *Gospel Messenger.*

GOSPEL MESSENGER

Okay! Come again! What was this—another SURPRISE task? Was it not *another something* I knew little about, or how to make it happen? Nevertheless, because Gerald had already produced the first copy, it gave me an idea of what it should look like—and except for the front page which showed a drawn map of PNG—all the rest of the magazine was simply to be done on a typewriter.

This was another incident of not having much choice in the matter, so from there, *by the Lord's help,* I began doing the best I could with what was available to do the job. The contents of the magazine included an editorial, testimonies, poems, a Bible study, and other articles of interest. Once I got started, I really enjoyed all that needed to be done to complete the task. I also began inquiring about how to make headings in different print from what I could do on the typewriter. It was at the *Swiss Missionary print shop* that I learned about press-on lettering and other things that would help improve the looks of the publication, but all this was so new to me. I also began to cut out pictures to add to it, trying to be as creative as I knew how. However, I could only do those extra things after *John Davolt* began to do the printing for me. He had some skill and equipment to do that, but until then it all had to be done on a spirit duplicator or mimeograph machine—I forget which! (In those days there were no computers or copy-machines available to produce a colorful, professional-looking job—except possibly in business offices—so I simply did the best I could with what was available to us!) Getting the English copy ready for printing was only one part of the job, for then it had to be translated into Pidgin as well. After that, the translated text had to be prepared for printing in the same way. It was quite a task, and usually had a deadline attached to it as well. All this kept me very busy, and sometimes I had to make the run to Mt. Hagen to get the printing done (in our little Suzuki) all by myself! On one such 3-hr. trip, an incident took place which was both frustrating and humorous—as well as something that made me very thankful!

Upon coming to the junction of the roads going to Ialibu and to Mendi, some policemen were there checking the cars as they came through the area. I was stopped and asked to show my driver's license. Because I couldn't locate my license in my purse immediately, I got unnerved and excited as I kept frantically searching in my purse to find it! All the while the policeman stood there patiently waiting as I was searching. Then a local woman with mental problems came from among the crowd of people gathered at the junction, and began banging on the hood of my vehicle. This drew away the attention of the policeman as he tried to stop the disturbance she was making. Finally he just waved for me to go on my way without further waiting to look at my license. What a relief, for I still had not found it! However, when I got home, I not only found the license, but when I took a *close look* at it, I discovered that it had expired! Wow! I was really thankful to find that out at home, instead of in the presence of that policeman! As you might guess, I took care of that matter as soon as I could after that! The lady with the mental problem proved to be a *blessing in disguise* to me that day!

In the meantime, Daniel had also been called upon to do another special job—something he had done many times before. For him, it was another building assignment, but this was much different from all the rest.

BUILDING the CHURCH and SCHOOL at LAE

Through the years Daniel had built many buildings at different stations. These included houses we lived in, houses for teachers, large school classrooms, outstation churches, clinic buildings, etc. Now this was the biggest assignment of all! It was to build a large, big-city church building in the coastal city of *Lae*, in the *Morobe Province*. That is where Gerald and Roana Bustin were living at the time, and this was to be EBM's first big-city outreach beyond the Highlands Provinces. A house had already been built for the Bustins, but now they were ready for a church building, a building for their ACE school, and a sizable toilet block as well.

Lae was quite a long distance from Mendi, but the trip could be made over the *Highlands Highway*, which went all the way from the Highland Provinces to the coast. However, I would need to remain at home in Mendi while Daniel was working there, so we would once again be temporarily separated for a matter of weeks.

When the job was finally completed and ready for the dedication, Roana secretly planned for me to fly to Lae and spend a few days there with Daniel for the occasion. That was a rather scary thing for me to do—especially since I would be flying on a regional airline that tended to have flight problems quite frequently. Many people completely avoided using that particular airline for that reason. However, since no flight was available on the national *Air Niugini Airline* at that particular time, I took the only other flight that was available, and experienced the close presence of the Lord all the way there. For one thing, while the weather was very threatening at that time, our flight had a smooth flight all the way. Flying at a low altitude, I could see stormy rain clouds off in the distance on both the right and left sides of the plane, but we were in the sunshine all the way. Then my attention was also drawn to a portion of a mountainside where there might have been a landslide, leaving part of it dry and barren, without any trees. It was there that I saw in the sunshine a portion of a rainbow, and just the sight of it caused me to fully relax and enjoy the entire trip. I was reassured that the Lord was truly there with me, and I would be safe.

Roana picked me up at the airport, and when we arrived at the house, she secretly escorted me into the house through the back door and had me wait unseen until the men came in for the evening meal after the day's work. When Daniel came into the kitchen, I simply stepped out into view and nonchalantly said, *"Hi!"*...just as though I had been there all the time! What a shock and *BIG SURPRISE* it was for Daniel to see me standing there in the kitchen—just as he was about to sit down to the table to eat! Of course, we then exchanged warm and loving greetings before we began the meal. Needless to say, we greatly enjoyed the rest of that special time together there with the Bustins. We stayed with them for the dedication of the church on Sunday, and then it was time for us to get back to Mendi.

MT. HAGEN, WESTERN HIGHLANDS

By now it was 1984, when we had another *big SURPRISE* revealed to us. This time we were being asked to fill in for *John and Sharon Davolt* and family at the fairly new *Mt. Hagen Church* during their year of furlough. Many new converts were a part of this church which met for services in a rented room of a building located in the town. (This room was also used on special occasions for voting purposes or other town functions lasting until very late on Saturday nights, and on Sunday mornings when we went for worship, we often found it very dirty and nasty with trash and the remains of *betel nut chewing—making it extremely undesirable for our church services!) Later Daniel built a lovely stone wall at the edge of the house property and nicely fixed up the space under the house where we lived, and that became our place of worship. Our living quarters were on the second level.

*(Chewing betel nut is a nasty sort of habit requiring the need to spit out the juice just like when chewing tobacco. However, the spittle from betel-nut is blood-red, rather than brown like tobacco juice. Truly the result is very disgusting! The effect on the mouth and teeth is likewise very unattractive, leaving its red stains in the mouth and on the teeth. As time goes on, users of betel nut often suffer from deterioration of their teeth and cancerous sores in their mouths.)

We were at the Mt. Hagen Church only one year, but it was truly a *wonderful* year. Daniel, of course, was then serving again as a pastor, and I helped along with the music—and still continuing on with producing the *Gospel Messenger* as well. The young couples of the church wanted very much to have a choir, so even though I was by then losing some of my vocal strength, at their request I did my best to assist them in learning and singing together many songs to praise and honor the Lord. We even made a tape of some of our songs, and on a couple occasions one of our songs was heard on the radio. Though the quality of the singing was not at all superb, the hearts of the singers truly loved the Lord. Both the *LORD* and *the singers* were blessed by their songs of praise and worship!

During that year in Mt. Hagen, the Church grew greatly in number as well as in the depth of understanding of the truths of God's Word. Many times we were called upon to give godly counsel to young Christians in the church who were having struggles in their homes because of unsaved spouses or other family members. Truly God was our helper even in times of weariness or diminishing physical and emotional strength. While there, Daniel also spent much time visiting at the local hospital, sharing the gospel with many people—both in the hospital and with those clustered around outside the hospital. He used a little booklet without words, but with pictures that told the story of man's need for a Savior, and of Jesus, God's Son, who came to this earth to be that Savior. Many gathered around to see the pictures and hear the story being shared with them.

Daniel's prison ministry was also continued at the prison of that area. Then one evening he had *a live encounter* with a prisoner that frightened all of us.

ENCOUNTER with an ARMED CAR THIEF

What happened was this: Our car and the church van were both under the house—where we also had the church services. A gate leading from the road that goes past our house into our driveway was always kept closed after dark. On this evening, however, it was still open because Daniel was planning to go away a bit later in the evening. Suddenly, he heard a noise under the house, and the sound of tires crunching on the gravel. Thinking someone was coming in the drive, he got up to see who it was. Instead, as he looked more closely at the vehicle that was there, he saw it was our own car that was being pushed out through the gate onto the road—headed toward the main road past the front of our house. Quickly he ran outside, yelling to us in the house, *"Someone is stealing our car. Call the police!"*

Immediately I did so—(but no police ever came, even throughout the whole ordeal!) The thief was trying to start the car, but was not able to; then Daniel threw a stone through the front side window, and reached into the car to undo some wires to make it *impossible* for them to start it. As these things were going on, Daniel discovered one of the men had a rifle, as he had made a shot on the ground near Daniel's feet. Then, watching for the right chance, Daniel turned quickly and grabbed hold of the rifle, trying to wrestle it out of the man's hand. Another man must have found our pocket knife on the dashboard tray of the car, for it was later found to be missing, and both of Daniel's hands had cuts near where he was grasping the rifle. As the struggle continued, Daniel's foot slipped on the pavement, and someone stomped him in his stomach, causing him to lose his grip on the gun. Still the men did not give up and run away, but after chasing away other observers, the man with the rifle held it up to the window of another vehicle that had stopped to see what was going on. He waved the gun back and forth in front of the driver of that vehicle, trying to get him to get out of the vehicle so he could use it to escape. Observing all this, Daniel saw another chance to try getting the rifle—which he did—and this time he held on tenaciously, finally getting the gun out of the man's hand. Then, running back to the house with it, he again told us to call the police. It was then that we noticed Daniel's eye was blackened, his glasses were gone, and there was blood on both his hands. (The glasses got crushed when Daniel slipped and fell.) A friend was there with Joy at this time, but when Joy saw her Daddy with a black eye and cut hands she really cried! As you can imagine, all of us in the house were frightened and praying about all that was going on—even though from there we could not see all the action. Quickly then, Daniel returned to the scene; but by then the men had all disappeared into the bush, and our car was left there at the side of the road! With the help of some of the observers, the car was finally pushed back to its place under the house where it was safe inside the locked gate! Now, however, it was in need of some repairs!

WOW! What an ordeal! What Daniel did seemed to be outrageously dangerous, but later he told us that he had felt no fear during the whole ordeal. The presence of the Lord was there in the darkness of the evening helping him in his struggle with the criminals. Later that same evening he took the gun to the police station, personally reporting to them what had happened, for they had never shown up in answer to our calls.

After things calmed down again, Daniel went to the local hospital to have the cuts on his hands sewed up and dressed. As the nurse was working on him, he made the statement, *"We need to pray for the man who did this!"*

To that the nurse—who was a Christian lady who attended our church, replied, *"What? Pray for him!"*

"Yes," Daniel said, *"He has a great need!"* And so…, we did pray for him—and for all the men involved in the incident! In fact, the people of the church were really moved when they saw Daniel's black eye and his injured hands, and at Daniel's request, they joined in praying earnestly for those men.

Shortly after this happened, news came that it was a well-known criminal named *Joseph Pai Mek* (with 17 counts against him), who had been the leader of those who has stolen our vehicle. By this time, however, he had been caught, and having escaped from the prison, he went to the home of a Pentecostal pastor whom he knew. There he repented of his sins, and according to a report on the radio, he was going to be baptized. Believing his conversion to be genuine, the authorities then released him. Soon after that he came to our church with several other Christian men, and together they sang a song during our service. It was at that time that he apologized to Daniel and to the church for the wrong he had done, stating that when he took the car, he had no idea that it belonged to a missionary! Sometime later, however, when a new authority came into power at the police headquarters, Joseph was again sent back to prison, considering all the *many crimes* he had done against society.

(Does it pay to pray for those who do wrong to us? It surely does! God is always faithful in dealing with those for whom we pray! Let's not give up on anyone who needs to know Jesus Christ as Savior—even though they be criminals!)

Finally, the time came for the Davolt family to return to PNG and take their place in Mt. Hagen once again. About that same time, we were again presented with another overwhelming *SURPRISE request.* This time we were being asked to *leave* the Highlands of PNG altogether! That is, we were being asked to transfer to the *capital city of Port Moresby,* which is located in the *Central Province,* down along the southern coast. There we would be representatives for EBM and the PNG Bible Church—where to the present there had never been any EBM missionaries. *Would we be willing to go there—*even *to that HOT, dry, coastal climate?*

LEFT: Daniel with Joseph Pia Mek who stole our car

BELOW:
Young Christian mothers with their babies on the day for Baby Dedications —NINE of them!

BELOW:
A partial group of the Christians at the Mt. Hagen Bible Church

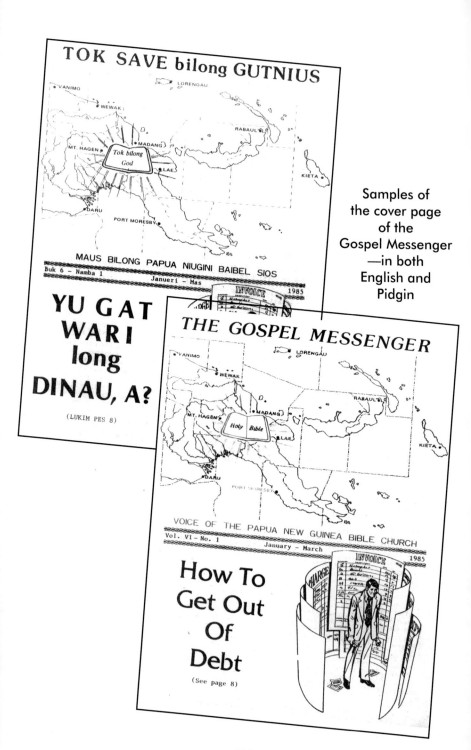

TOK SAVE bilong GUTNIUS

Tok bilong God

MAUS BILONG PAPUA NIUGINI BAIBEL SIOS

Buk 6 - Namba 1   Janueri - Mas   1985

YU GAT WARI long DINAU, A?

(LUKIM PES 8)

THE GOSPEL MESSENGER

Holy Bible

VOICE OF THE PAPUA NEW GUINEA BIBLE CHURCH

Vol. VI - No. 1   January - March   1985

How To Get Out Of Debt

(See page 8)

Samples of
the cover page
of the
Gospel Messenger
—in both
English and
Pidgin

Chapter 10

CAPITAL CITY

PORT MORESBY / GEREHU

(OUR FINAL YEARS in PNG)

Once again, by seeking to know the mind of God through prayer, we soon knew that this was God's will for us to accept the challenge offered to us. Actually, it was truly an honor for us to be entrusted with this new assignment, so it was not long, therefore, until we were preparing ourselves for this big transition.

The city of *Port Moresby* was the largest city in Papua New Guinea. It was also the center of their *National Government*, and where their largest buildings and the spectacular *Parliament Building* were located. It was the arrival and departure point for all the missionaries coming to or leaving PNG, and yet until this time, EBM had no missionary personnel to represent them there or to welcome the new missionaries when they came. However, there were already young men and women from the *highlands* PNG Bible Churches and schools living there, who were attending the *University of Papua New Guinea* (UPNG) or working in the city; and together these youth formed the nucleus of what later became the *first* PNG Bible Church in the city of Port Moresby.

Yes…living and working in this *capital city* would surely be another exciting and challenging change for us—with numerous hurdles to be faced and overcome.

Here is the list of those hurdles—which, one by one, the Lord helped us to overcome, making them stepping stones to outreach and ministry development rather than hindrances.

#1) There was no available housing, or mission property of any kind on which to build.

#2) There was no church building where we could gather to worship. Presently, the only a meeting place the students had was a University classroom.

#3) For me in particular, maneuvering a vehicle through the city would be a challenge!

#4) For our food supply, there would be no gardens to supply us with *fresh vegetables or fruits* as we were so accustomed to enjoying in the Highlands. Food of any kind would be expensive.

#5) We would be completely separated from the rest of the EBM missionary family.

#6) Where would Joy continue her schooling—*unless* I became her ACE supervisor again?

In spite of all these differences and uncertainties, the Lord again went before us and prepared the way ahead of us. For one thing, it was just about this same time that some of the young men of our mission who were already living and working there in the city, had *finally* been able to locate and procure a property where the PNG Bible Church could develop its ministry and begin building a house for a missionary family to live in. Therefore, it was not long before negations were completed and documents were in place, for this piece of ground in the area called *GEREHU* to become the focal point for starting a house-building project. That took care of *hurdles #1 & #2!* With those issues in place, it was soon discovered that just a short walking-distance away from the new property was also a *Baptist Mission* that had an ACE School already in operation. That meant that Joy could possibly continue her ACE school curriculum there with them, and *I would not have to personally supervise her at home! How wonderful that would be for her, and for me as well!* When contact was made, and the arrangement was agreed upon, that was *hurdle #6* already crossed, and we were so thankful for that!

Then the matter of *immediate* housing—where we would live while our house was being built—was also providentially solved even before we went to Port Moresby, for we had learned that there was a wonderful way to solve that problem! In the main towns or cities of PNG, it was quite customary for ex-patriots (as foreigners from Australia, Great Britain, New Zealand, USA, etc. were called), to advertise their homes for someone to occupy and care for them during their time of leave from PNG. Such houses were called *leave-houses*. Now that we needed a place to live, and having little possessions to move about from place to place, we answered some of these advertisements, and in that way we were provided with very nice places to live—temporarily. What a blessing! In each house all that was required of us while living there, was to pay the utilities and take care of plants or animals—as needed. No rent was required otherwise. In all, we lived in four different *leave-houses* during the time Daniel was building our house. The time we stayed in each one varied from 4 weeks to 3 months, and it was actually *fun* for me to experience life in such a variety of settings. At some places we kept flowers watered, at others we fed dogs, and in all of these houses we were quite comfortable with the arrangements as provided.

It was in the last of these houses where we stayed that the Lord supplied another of the needs I would be facing while living so distantly separated from all the rest of our fellow-missionaries. The owners of this house were *Arabs* from the *West Bank* of *Jordan*. The husband was in PNG working with the *World Health Organization*. It was in the bedroom where we slept in that home, that I noticed a Bible-study booklet lying on the bedside stand that was entitled, *The Practice of Godliness* by Jerry Bridges. That really took my attention.

"Wow," I thought, *"these people must be Christians!"* Their house was very special, with some very unique pieces of furniture and numerous interesting things in plain view in the living room, and throughout the house. I did my best to keep everything in perfect order as we had found it. Then, just before we began the process of moving out, a knock came on the door. When we opened the door, we were surprised to see it was the owners themselves—*Odi and Helen Habash*—who had knocked at the door of their own house! They simply smiled at us and asked, *"May we come in?"*

Then, introducing themselves to us again, they said, *"We just want to let you know that we are back from our leave, but we will give you ample time to vacate the house. We will be ready to move back in tomorrow when you have gone."*

They were so nice! But the friendship between us did not end there, for when I asked Helen about the Bible-study booklet I saw in the bedroom, she told me that it was the booklet she and other ladies were studying in the weekly prayer and Bible-study time for *International Christian Women* living there in the city. How happy I was to learn about this, and it was not long until I was joining in with them for times of spiritual fellowship. Oh, how wonderful it was to see how God went before us to supply just what I needed for spiritual growth and Christian fellowship—in addition to our weekly church services. I was so thankful how the Lord led in this way—crossing *the 5th hurdle* so beautifully. Later on, I was able to host the Bible-study meeting at our house occasionally as well.

With Daniel being very busy in the process of building our house, I was left with the responsibility of being the *Liaison Officer* for EBM there in the city. Many times there were official matters that had to be taken care of between the Government and the Mission. Until now there had been no one in Port Moresby to take care of those matters, but that was one of the things we were now expected to do. That meant many trips to the *Immigrations* office building, where work-permits for our missionaries were issued. Sometimes having to stand in line for hours at a time—yet not being served, and finally told to return on the next day—became a real trial to *everybody* needing service! That is where I learned about what was called *tunnel-vision!* That description sounded amusing to me, yet it was not very funny to everyone standing in lines next to the counter. You see, one day as quite a few people were waiting *a long time* for someone to come through the door at the end of the space behind the counter, we were all getting edgy and wanting to be served. Then finally, *a man did actually come through the door!* Now our wait would soon be over, and we would soon be served—*so we thought!* But lo, the man did not come to the counter and serve anyone at all! Instead, he walked the full length of the counter to the other end—all the time looking straight ahead—not responding to any-one even though different ones called out to him to come serve them. Instead, he went right back through the second door and out of sight again—not stopping to serve anyone or even *look* at them! Those of us who were waiting could do nothing more than to wait some more—or go home! When that happened, someone waiting in line made the remark, *"That man has tunnel-vision!"* Ha! Ha! I thought that was funny! But some of the people there surely did not think so—for they showed signs of anger and frus-tration instead! Quite likely many others *felt* that way, as well! Nevertheless, it was not *always* like that, and as for me, I just kept going back until *finally* I would get my business taken care of.

Living in the city also meant that I had to learn to find my way around through much heavier traffic than I had ever driven in before. In the Highlands, driving on the mountain roads was completely different—and even there for many years I had not driven at all. In PNG, the driver sits on the right side of the car to drive, and drives on the left side of the road. In the highlands that difference did not propose much of a problem, because much of the time on the open road you would have the whole road to your-self. However, where there is lots of traffic, as in the city, it does make a *big* difference! At one intersection where I had to cross a busy lane of traffic to make a right turn without the aid of a traffic signal, I would often be gripped by fear that I would not be able to negotiate the turn safely. That really bothered me.

Then one day the Holy Spirit seemed to be saying to me, *"Helen, do you see all these other drivers who are negotiating this same turn you are so fearful of making? Quite likely many of those drivers do not even know me, so they do not ask for my help. If they can do it without my help, surely can do it with my help! I am right here with you to help you do it safely, so trust me!"*

With that, my spirit was calmed, and I became relaxed and peaceful at that junction from that time on! Once again, I praise the Lord for His faithfulness in teaching me another lesson in trusting Him for *everything* I need—solving the *#3 hurdle* with peace and calmness!

As for our food supply, we simply learned to eat whatever we could get in the market—though at a higher price—and what we could buy in the stores. Occasionally we did take a drive up into a coastal mountainous area where fresh produce that did not grow in the city-area climate could be bought more reasonably-priced, and that was a real treat. This issue was *hurdle #4*, which we had to accept as it was!

After being in our new house for a couple years, and having moved our church services from the University classroom to the space under our house, *(hurdle #3),* we were enjoying our ministry and the people that filled the worship space week after week. We also had wonderful times of prayer, worship, and fellowship in our home quite frequently as well. Eventually we had a baptismal service for new converts who were now a part of our congregation. For a place to baptize, a large water-tank—like those tanks used to catch rain water for drinking—was placed in our back yard and filled with water to be used as a baptismal pool. There was great joy among the people at these special occasions!

Here in Port Moresby we again visited the prison in the area to share the gospel with the prisoners. It was there that Daniel once again met the man, Joseph Pia Mek, who had stolen our car in Mt. Hagen. At this time he was not doing well, because he was being badly treated there in the prison. Many prisoners hated him, beating up on him, and making life miserable for him. As for his faith in God, we were not sure how well he was doing at that time, for we did not have opportunity to talk personally with him. However, we realized he was greatly in need of our continued prayers, so we kept on praying for him.

THE NOISE in the NIGHT

Another incident of our car being stolen occurred while we were in Port Moresby. This time, however, there was a tall wire fence all around the church property, and the gate was closed securely. During the early morning hours of the night, Daniel heard a loud *"BANG"*! Then there was another, and another, until there were six in all. Daniel thought someone in the neighborhood must be having a fight and breaking up things in their house. However, when we got up in the morning, we discovered that our Subaru was missing from under our house, and the fence had been cut open to take the vehicle out of our yard. How shocking! During that time, one of our Christian young couples *(Morgan and Regina)* was living in the small apartment on the ground-floor of our house. Morgan himself was a policeman, and both he and Regina had also heard the loud noise in the night. Then someone reported to us that our vehicle *might* be found down the small road leading to the sewage disposal plant, so together Morgan and Daniel went out looking for it there. And sure enough, that is where they found it! But oh, what a sight it was! Not only were the tires missing, but every wheel was also missing, and every glass—front, back, and both sides—was shattered to bits! (Apparently, that was what was heard during the night!) Even the upholstery was ripped off the inside of the front doors, and a supply of gospel tracts that was left in the car was scattered all over the ground just outside the car as well. What a sight the Subaru was to behold in that condition!! I could hardly believe what I was seeing! It almost made you feel sick to think that someone would do such a malicious thing to a good vehicle—and for what reason! I cannot remember how the vehicle was brought back to the church property to be repaired, but there it sat in our back yard, waiting for the repair job to be done. Then Daniel went out searching for an old vehicle of the same make and model so that he could take parts from it for the repairs. What he found was at the police station—a light blue Subaru of the same model—just what he needed! Soon after making the purchase from the police, Daniel had all the repairs and replacements in place, and our 'good ole Subaru' was ready to go again! How thankful we were to have found the stolen vehicle, and what a relief it was that we did not have to spend *lots* of money to get it back on the road again! We praised the Lord for that!

THE DRAMA:
"I DREAMED I SEARCHED HEAVEN for YOU"

Here again at Port Moresby, as in all the other places we had worked, the young people of the church wanted to sing together as a choir. After getting started and doing some practice together, I suggested that we try to do a musical drama based on the song, *"I Dreamed I Searched Heaven for You."* We had done this drama years before — when we lived in Michigan, and more recently at PNGBI.

Because we needed more help to make the drama truly effective, we invited anyone interested at the Baptist church (where Joy was going to school) to join with us for the drama. (They had some *very good* singers there.) The school principal, John Wesley, his wife (who was one of Joy's teachers), and a few others accepted our invitation and cooperated with us. It was a blessing to us, and also to them, to have these times of mutual fellowship between us. We enjoyed the experience of working together in this way.

In the drama, the platform at the front of the church was to represent *Heaven*. In order to make it more impressive, a beautiful background scene was painted on two large, white bed sheets sewn together, and then hung at the back of the platform. A young teen-age boy did the painting on *the flat roof of his house*. All I had to give him for an idea of what to paint on it was a small slide picture from my *Pilgrim's Progress* slides of that story, but he did a marvelous job of coming up with a beautiful painting, using his own ideas as well. He painted a golden street lined with beautiful trees, and a bright, shining throne at the distant end of the street—with an angel in the scene as well. It was a spectacular painting!

Since our congregation was still meeting under our house, and we had no suitable place to present the drama, we did our first and only practice at the Baptist church. Everyone present was deeply touched and moved by the time the drama was completed. The Spirit of God manifested His presence in a very special way that night. Earlier we had gained permission to do the drama in the open forum of the University of PNG, so there is where we had our first public presentation. There rows of seats surrounded the open floor of the forum, with a balcony area at the top of the steps on one side. This balcony served as the *Heaven* area, with the piano, choir, and singers on the steps below the balcony and in the center of the floor space. At the beginning, when the piano music began, there was some heckling by some of the University students, but as the drama began and proceeded, the heckling stopped and again there was truly a moving of the Holy Spirit in our midst. The drama included many songs—many of which were sung by the choir, but there were also duets, solos, and quartet numbers as well. Here is the program of the drama as it unfolded:

I DREAMED I SEARCHED HEAVEN for YOU

22nd April, 1985

Prelude: (Instrumental or Solo)	*The Holy City*
Welcome and Introduction:	PNG Bible Church Pastor
Pearly White City	
Where We'll Never Grow Old	Combined Singing Group
Scripture & Prayer:	Baptist Church Pastor
In the Sweet By and By	Congregational Song
I Dreamed I Searched Heaven for You	
	Reader: John Wesley and Singing Group
When the Roll is Called Up Yonder	Singing Group
Bringing in the Sheaves	Quartet
I Bowed on My Knees and Cried Holy	Solo
Where the Gates Swing Outward Never	Singing Group
I Dreamed I Searched Heaven for You	
	Reader and Singing Group
Mansion Over the Hilltop	Baptist Church Girls' Group
The Great Judgment Morning	Singing Group
Jewels	Children's Group
Gathering Buds	Double Duet (Two Couples)
I Dreamed I Searched Heaven for You	
	Reader and Singing Group
O, I Would Not Want to Miss It!	Singing Group
Suppertime	PNG Bible Church Girls' Group
Will the Circle Be Unbroken?	Quartet & Singing Group
When the Saints Go Marching In	Singing Group
Going Home	Solo: Joy Glick / Singing Group
When We All Get to Heaven	Singing Group
Will We Search Heaven for You?	Singing Group
Why Not Tonight? (Invitation Song)	Everyone Singing

As the drama was progressing, quite a few of our group and some of the singers had been gathering on the balcony which represented *Heaven,* but some were also being rejected by the angel at the entrance—especially during the song, *"The Great Judgment Morning."* Then near the close of the drama, an invitation was given for those of the audience who were trusting Jesus as their Savior and were ready for *Heaven,* to come join with those going to the balcony when the song *"When the Saints Go Marching In"* was being sung. Also, anyone who wanted to come to Christ Jesus to be saved right then—to be made ready for Heaven, so as not to be missing when that final day comes—could join them, too. A number responded, but one individual was so moved that he came out of the crowd and ran right up the steps to the top balcony where *Heaven* was, passing all the rest. I guess we will never know who, or how many, truly trusted the Lord Christ as their Savior as a result of that presentation; but we do know that the Holy Spirit was there working among the crowd that night.

Standing in front of the painting done for the Drama—
"I Dreamed I Searched Heaven for You"

Besides this presentation at the University, there were two other doors opened to us to give the drama. One was at an *Assembly of God Church*, but I can not remember where the other one was. God was faithful to bless the drama at each place where it was presented. We were so thankful for the help of the Lord in making it possible for our church family and those who helped us to reach out to more people of the city in that way.

A BUILDING for the PNG BIBLE CHURCH CONGREGATION in GEREHU

After all this had taken place, we finally began the church-building project for our congregation on the mission property—right next to the house Daniel had built earlier. It was not built promptly after the completion of the house because there were not enough funds to build it. However, as time went on, funds were raised and set aside for this next project, and in 1987 a church building was completed, and we began worshipping there instead of under our house. I cannot remember what month we made that change, but the dedication was held in November of that year.

First, however, I must tell you of something that happened when the church was being built. I remember clearly that the project was in progress in May of 1987, during the time the annual Ladies' Retreat was being held in the Highlands. I usually was not privileged to attend these meetings after we moved to Port Moresby, because a costly plane fare was needed to make the trip. However, this year I had been invited to speak once again, so I went for the retreat. It was on Saturday evening, that in the message being given, I was stressing to the ladies the importance of trusting the Lord for His grace to help us in *all* circumstances in our lives—whether good or bad. I cannot remember the Scripture being used, but that was one of the main points of the message. It was at the close of the service, when *Brenda Rose—the Field Leader's wife—* came immediately to me, gently asking me to come aside so she could talk with me. (Right away I wondered *why* she wanted to speak to me so urgently.) We then went out of the church, and I was told that she had received a message for me from Port Moresby, saying that my husband, Daniel, had a serious fall while working on the church, and he was now in the hospital! *WOW, what a shock that was!* And did that bit of news ever give me a chance to *practice* what I had just preached to the ladies!

Immediately, then, I made personal phone contact with someone there in Port Moresby to find out more. In so doing, I was told that *Daniel will be alright.* He did have a hard fall and was in the hospital, but *he did not want me to shorten my stay and come home before the retreat was over.* The men there had special prayer for him, and he was presently doing quite well in spite of the fall. And so it was—I stayed until the end of the retreat, continuing on with my assignment *only by help of a special touch from the Lord.* In so doing, this was a demonstration to the ladies of the power of God to give peace and stability, even in the midst of unfavorable circumstances—just as I was trying to teach to the ladies! God was so faithful to stand by me at that time! And He does the same for *all of us* as we fully trust in Him at all times!

It wasn't until I got back home that I learned how the fall had occurred. I'm not good at describing details about how a building is being built, so I cannot fully explain what caused him to fall; but to put it briefly, he fell approximately 11 feet, landing on *his seat* and making a deep dent in the soft ground below! No bones were broken, and he recovered from the trauma quite quickly. And surprisingly, even *something good* came out of that fall!

For years Daniel had had a problem with pain in his back—especially when sometimes his one leg would become shorter than the other from an imbalance in carrying weight and walking over uneven surfaces. However, after this fall, that problem with his back seemed to all but disappear! Is that not in keeping with the Scripture, which says, "*All things work together for good, to them that love God and to them who are the called according to His purpose."*? Once again, *to God be all the glory for His way of helping us face life's problems with peace and rejoicing instead of frustration!* Amen!

OUR HOUSE—A GUEST HOUSE

So many good and encouraging things were taking place in the ministry there in the capital city. Our congregation was growing, and our youth were reaching out into new areas in the region. Some of these areas became regular outstation preaching points of the Port Moresby Church District. There were also more new missionaries coming in from USA, heading to the Highlands to be working at one of the original EBM stations there, or locating at new outreach areas of the Highlands. Our house in Gerehu became the stopping place for those coming and going, and part of our responsibility of being there was to *be their host and hostess* and *meet their overnight lodging and transportation needs* while in the city. I enjoyed my part of that very much! On one occasion there were two families—possibly 12 in all, arriving at the airport at one time. With the large number of passengers, plus all their luggage, there was no way we could bring them all to our house without making numerous trips with our Subaru. In that case, we requested the use of the Baptist Church bus, and they willingly honored our request by giving us permission to use it. Having a place for all these guests to spend the night was another matter, but as I recall, some way or other we were able to meet that need as well. While living there in Gerehu, I did not have regular house-girls to help me as I had at Tambul and Pabarabuk, so Joy and I worked together doing the household chores—cooking, laundry, cleaning, etc., along with the mission and church responsibilities. We were usually kept very busy. For a period of time (which I do not recall clearly), one of the girls of the church family, Alice Yaite, stayed in our home and became our close friend. To her, and to many of the young couples of the church body, we were like *"Mom and Dad,"* and Joy was like their younger sister.

On one occasion we met some new missionaries coming to work with EBM, and because they had only a layover of several hours before going on to the highlands, we brought them to our house for a light snack and an opportunity to see the location of our work there in the city. We were having such an enjoyable visit together that the missionary couple forgot about the time of their departure until there was very little time left to get them back to the airport! Nevertheless, when we finally realized the lateness of the hour, we left the house with haste and got them back to the airport—*just in time!* They did *not* miss their flight.

For one of our faithful missionary families, however, there came a time of departure from the field that was filled with great sorrow. It was the death of *Marilyn Sturtevant* that caused her husband, *Steve*, and two children—*Jason and Stephanie*, to unexpectedly return to the States. Marilyn had been experiencing serious physical problems, but after special prayers for her healing, she responded with great improvement and was beginning to function normally again in the home. Several days later, however, she once again became ill, and this time she did not recover. Her passing was a heavy loss to her family, to her ministry with the ACE School, and to the entire EBM missionary family. When Daniel and I got the news in Port Moresby, we were not both able to go to the Highlands for the funeral, so I went alone. After the sad farewell and memorial service, Marilyn was laid to rest right there in a special hillside area of the Pabarabuk Station—where she had been serving the Lord for a number of years.

(Marilyn previously worked as a single missionary with another mission group before her marriage to Steve Sturtevant. She was an outstanding scholar of both Greek and Hebrew. In 1979 she and Steve returned to PNG with their two children to begin the ACE school for missionary children. Marilyn was truly a well-loved missionary. She also wrote a book entitled *Orchids on a Waste*

Hillside that told of her life and experiences during her years as a missionary.)

(Other members of our missionary family who went to be with the Lord while in PNG are *Dale Mahan*, *Tracy Rose* and Lenita Bustin. In each case, the loss of their presence as a part of the missionary family was very keenly felt by all of us—as well as by their personal families both on the field and at home in USA. Likewise, the PNG Bible Church family and personal PNG friends of each one mourned for them, sharing lovingly in their grief and loss. For all of us, our hope of Heaven is now more keenly alive for us because of those of our number who are already there waiting for us!)

~~~~ SOME SPECIAL GUESTS ~~~~

ABOVE:
Two Mennonite couples
from Plain City, OH,
and a son-in-law of
one of the couples

RIGHT:
Armon & Elong
Seimsen Wycliffe
missionaries from
California with Joy

After Marilyn's funeral, I remained there at Pabarabuk until Steve and his two children were ready to return to USA; then John Davolt flew the four of us to Port Moresby in the mission plane. From there Steve, Jason, and Stephanie went back to their grieving family and friends in USA. I did my best to comfort the sad little girl and her older brother as we traveled that flight together. Their loss was so great!

Besides these incidents with missionaries coming and going, we had some other visitors, too. Daniel's brother Earl and wife Thelma came to visit us—as well as Thelma's sister, Esther Hershey—who was then working at Pabarabuk in the Highlands. Part of their time was spent with us at Gerehu, but it was so very hot! They were glad to be able to go on to the Highlands where Esther lived, where it was much cooler and more comfortable. I do not remember the exact time of their visit, but I believe it was while Daniel was building the church. Another time a California couple—*Armon* and *Elong Seimsen*, who were working with Wycliffe Translators, stopped by for a visit. Then in return we visited them in their California home on one of our furlough trips back to USA. For quite a few years afterwards we shared newsletters with each other, even after neither we nor they were any longer in PNG.

At another time two Mennonite couples from Plain City, OH, visited us as well. They had come to visit some family members who were also working with Wycliffe in PNG. While staying at the MAF Missionary Hostel in town, they heard that missionaries from Ohio were living in the area, so they decided to look us up and make this visit. It was always exciting for us to become acquainted with new people—especially when they had some kind of connection with people we knew in USA. During our visit with these couples, we discovered that they were personally acquainted with some of Daniel's relatives in the Plain City area of Ohio. That was very interesting!

When visitors came to our house, we would usually take them on a small tour around the coastal area of the city. From where we lived, we could not see the waters of the Pacific that surrounded the Island of New Guinea, but we did not have far to go to see fabulous views of those beautiful *waters*. One interesting sight along the way was the *Hanuabada Village* which was built over the waters—where houses with walkways between them were built on supporting stilts extending deep into the water below. We would also pass the squatters' settlement, where make-shift houses were scattered over the hillsides overlooking the beautiful blue waters. They were in sharp contrast to the tall, modern apartment buildings, hotels, banks, business and government buildings of downtown Port Moresby—which also overlooked the same beautiful waters. Then there was the beach—where we would sometimes go with a picnic lunch—or even go wading a bit. Otherwise, we had little experience in/on the waters around Port Moresby. On one occasion, however, our Baptist missionary friend took us out for a ride in his small craft—his way of saying *"thank you"* to Daniel for building a special trailer to carry it to the waters. That was an unusual treat for us.

Our sight-seeing tours usually always included a brief stop at the spectacular *Parliament House*, where all government meetings are conducted. On one occasion we were invited to have a meal in the cafeteria there with one of the Christian Parliament members. He also took us inside the meeting room to observe the Parliament when it was in session. That was very interesting.

We also enjoyed having our fellow-missionaries from the Highlands spend some extra time with us when they were coming to or departing from the field for their furloughs, for we were all a part of *one, big missionary family!* We always truly enjoyed that—in addition to the warm friendship and times of fellowship we had with our national *"brothers and sisters"* in the Lord there in the city.

Scenes of
Hanuabada Village

A few of the
houses in the
Squatter's
Settlement

ABOVE: The beautiful unique Parliament Building
BELOW: Buildings in Downtown Port Moresby

A Hotel

A Bank

A Department Store

THE TALE of a BROKEN LEG

Time was marching on, and in September of 1987 a change came into our lives that played a big part in many things that happened in our lives after that—even to the present day. It was house-cleaning time for me, and being located right along a busy junction where there were a lot of cars passing by our house on the dusty, unpaved road, the cleaning task was a frequent necessity. In the hot climate with no air-conditioning, all the jalousie windows were open practically all the time, so dust quickly settled on everything in the house.

On this particular day—Friday, I had already taken things off the walls in the living-room and moved some of the furniture so I could wash down the walls. Then I stopped to prepare and eat our lunch. After I had finished eating, I went back to my job, but Daniel was still in the kitchen. (Joy was in school.) Placing my small step-stool under one of my lovely houseplants hanging from the ceiling in a macramé hanger, I took the sweeper hose in my hand to vacuum the hanger. Then, as I was reaching up with both hands—that is when it happened! What I had done wrong, I was not sure of—but the next thing I *knew,* I had fallen to the floor with a loud *"thump!"* Immediately I knew that something in my leg was broken!

I screamed out to Daniel, *"Come quick, Honey, I broke my leg!"*

I was in great pain! Quickly Daniel came, and sure enough, he could see that my foot was turned at an angle from my leg. What he did next I was completely unaware of, because I was in so much pain! He thought my foot was disjointed at the ankle, so he pulled hard to get it back in place. He *did* get it straightened out, but my pain continued, so the next thing to do was to get me to a doctor.

As I lay there, I began to feel sorry for whoever was going to have to carry me downstairs to the vehicle to take me wherever I had to go—because my weight was sufficient to make me a *heavy load* for anyone to carry! At this point Daniel again called our Baptist friends—Pastor *Ken Jenkins or John Wesley*—just up the road. One of them (I forget which) came quickly, and together he and Daniel laid me on the thick foam cushion we used on our couch and carried me down the steps to our Subaru station-wagon. At this point the Subaru conveniently became the ambulance that took me to the doctor and then to the hospital. At the Doctor's office, the doctor came out to the car to take a look, and then sent me directly to the hospital for x-rays. There I was taken out of the car, put on a stretcher, and taken into the hospital to get the x-rays. Then I was taken back to the car, put back on my foam mattress and taken back to the doctor. He then examined the x-rays and tried hard to re-set the small broken bone just above my ankle to get it back in place next to the other bone that was not broken. After putting a large cast on it, the doctor allowed both Daniel and I to sleep there in his office building that night. In the morning he sent me back to the hospital again for more x-rays. When we returned, he let me remain on the foam padding in the back of the car while he examined the new set of x-rays.

After the examination he shook his head, saying, *"That's not good enough! You will have to go South (to Australia) for surgery."*

However, because it would take time to arrange the flight and transfer to the hospital in Cairns, Australia, and there was no opening until Tuesday, he allowed me go home until those arrangements could be completed. I was glad about that, because it gave me time to make arrangements for Joy while we would be away. We were not sure then how long we would be away from home.

When I got home with the heavy cast on my leg, I had to make my way up the steps into our house by sitting on the step and lifting myself up one step at a time. To go to church on Sunday, I had to do the same going down, as well as back up again. In the house I moved about on my office chair, and was also able to do some of my work in the office on Saturday afternoon and Monday before leaving on Tuesday.

At the airport the biggest challenge lay before me, for the entrance into the airplane had to be made via steps from the ground—as many as 22 (or more) of them! There was no lift available, so the only way to accomplish that was to hop on one foot from step to step all the way to the top. Nevertheless, with the help of Daniel and an airline worker, I made it—and together the two of us enjoyed the flight all the way to Cairns, Australia!

In Cairns, it was a Catholic hospital to where I was taken for surgery. At the hospital, I was treated with great respect—almost as though I was one of *their own Catholic sisters!* After a week in the hospital following the surgery, I was released, but it was necessary for me to stay nearby for another 10 days so that the staples could be removed and a new cast put on my leg before returning home. During all this time, Daniel was there with me staying in a missionary hostel near the hospital, so the last 10 days we spent all our time together at the hostel. We had a wheelchair to use, so Daniel would take me out for rides in the nearby park. It was such a nice, peaceful place for such a stroll.

It was not until we looked at the x-rays that we actually saw what they had done in the surgery. Four small screws were put into the small broken bone at different angels, and one 3" long screw was put straight through my leg from outside to inside in order to pull the broken bone back in its place near the larger one. In six weeks the large screw was to be removed, but the smaller ones could be left there indefinitely—or removed after a year if they were irritating me as time went on.

It was a happy day for all of us when we arrived home again. Joy had baked a cake and decorated it with the words, *"Welcome home"* on it. While cumbered with a heavy cast, I had to move around the house to do my work on a wheel-chair for quite a while, and going up and down the steps was now a continual, difficult activity for me. (Before my fall, I was used to running up and down the steps most of the time!) In due time, however, when I was allowed to put a bit of weight on my leg, I started using a crutch—and though I was on my feet once again, life went on at a much slower pace!

It was during the time of this accident and recovery that our friend, *Helen Habash* (in whose *leave-house* we had lived while our house was being built), came to my rescue and helped me with some of my classes in the schools where we would go for *Religious Instruction classes*. I had learned to know her quite well through our Bible-study and prayer times together with many other international ladies, and now she was glad to help me in this way. She was such a blessing.

Also, during that time of recovery, our Ladies' Bible-study group was invited to the *American Ambassador's home* for an informal luncheon. Food was served on the patio surrounding the large pool at their modern, high-rise home overlooking the coastal area of Port Moresby. I felt somewhat embarrassed, not being able to move about very well among the people, but it was quite an honor to be welcomed there—even as I was. Daniel was there with me, and that helped me not to feel so self-conscious of my handicap at that time. The Ambassador's wife was one of the ladies who regularly attended our Ladies' Bible-study and prayer meetings.

As the year was coming to an end, we were now planning for the dedication of our new church. Some special guests from USA were planning to be there for that occasion. *Harold Schmul and William Gale*, both leading ministers of the Inter-church Holiness Movement, and *Gerald Bustin*—then General Secretary of EBM, were making this trip to PNG for this occasion. Also, *Mondopa Mini*—PNG Bible Church Chairman from the Highlands, was with them. Here again, being still quite handicapped and much in need of crutches, I was unable to function normally as a hostess. Nevertheless, I was learning the importance of doing my best—in spite of inconvenient circumstances.

By this time I had already traveled to the Highlands, to the Nazarene Hospital located at Kudjip. There the large cast was completely removed, and the large screw was removed from my leg. *Beverly Wickham,* our missionary nurse, accompanied me to the hospital for the surgery, then brought me back to Mt. Hagen, where I stayed a few days before returning to Port Moresby. It felt *so good* to get that huge cast off of my leg once again, making it so much easier for me to use the crutches as well.

As the year was closing in on us, another major change was also taking place. We had been looking forward to another furlough early in the following year, but instead it seemed that December of that year, 1987, was the best time for us to be leaving. While writing these last pages of *My Story, Part II*, I located a copy of the January-February issue of the *Mission Messenger,* (1988) and discovered a *Farewell Article* I had written just four weeks before we left our ministry in Papua New Guinea. I feel it would be very fitting to use that article to finalize *My Story, Part II* as well. The following photos were also a part of that same issue of the *Mission Messenger.* Here now are the photos with the article on the following pages…

UPDATE ON PORT MORESBY . . .

The nearly-completed church building at Port Moresby as it sits next to the house.

After a Sunday morning service in the new church.

A close-up of the sign identifying the Church.

Sunday School children on the outside of new church building.

GLICK FAMILY SAYS FAREWELL

The Port Moresby Church Choir and
part of the Congregation

Port Moresby P.N.G. Bible Church—
A Sunday morning congregation

Daniel, Brother Gerald and Brother Schmul on
the platform on Dedication Day (Nov. 8, 1987)
Daniel gives the financial report (debt free!)

Brother Gerald speaks to the Congregation
on Dedication Day, Nov. 8, 1987

UPDATE on PORT MORESBY CHURCH
and
FAREWELL

(From the Daniel Glick Family—November 1987)

Greetings to all the MISSION MESSENGER readers, from your missionaries and the congregation at Port Moresby.

You've heard little from this part of PNG during the past 2½ years, so it is time to let you know just what is happening here in the *"great city"* of Papua New Guinea, namely PORT MORESBY.

As usual, the area at present is quite dry and parched from lots of sunshine which is prevalent the year round. Cool breezes alleviate the intensity of the heat somewhat, and when the rains finally come in another month or two, that will help as well. In spite of the dryness, however, this is the season for delicious mangoes from the many mango trees all over the city. Beautiful bougainvilleas are in full bloom these days as well, which gives the city a touch of beauty in spite of the otherwise drab look of the general area. Other blossoming trees add their touch of beauty just now as well.

In GEREHU, the area where we live and where the PNG Bible Church is located, our family continues to "hold the fort" and carry on with the work that needs to be done here. On the 8th of November this year, the dedication service for our new church building was finally held. It was our aim to have the opening service when Brother Gerald Bustin, Brother Harold Schmul, and Brother William Gale arrived from USA, but when that time came, we still were not ready. However, a change in their departing schedule allowed more time for the completion of the church benches, so we were able to have the dedication just before they left PNG instead. (Bro. Gale was not present, however, because he had gone ahead of the others to Manila one week earlier.) There was still more work to be done at the time of the dedication, and now Daniel is busy working at those final finishing touches—like staining and varnishing the benches, putting up the fly and security screens, putting up the guttering, building the platform steps, etc. As for the painting, that will be done in due time, perhaps by the next missionary that follows us. There's also beautifying to be done outside, like planting flowers and shrubbery around the church, but that will have to be done when the rains come rather than now.

We thank God for the many encouraging things that have taken place in the church during the 2½ years we've been here in the city, but as a whole our congregation is much in need of a revival that will help them as individuals to put Christ first in *EVERY AREA* of their lives. Sometimes we could become very discouraged, but since we're not looking at circumstances, or people, or depending on our feelings, we rejoice *IN THE LORD* and praise Him for what He is doing here in this part of His vineyard. We do pray, however, that our people will open up their hearts and yield their lives completely to the Holy Spirit, so that they will not come short of the fullness of the blessings that God has for them as they serve Him in this place. It is a real challenge to live for Him in a city setting such as this, but many succumb to the temptations around them rather than recognize the challenge as one that could be a stepping stone for them to have a closer walk with the Lord.

Many guests have come and gone through the doors of our home during this year, and we've enjoyed having every one of them! Getting work permits, visas and visa extensions—and sometimes passports, for our missionary families has been a part of my work here, and I've enjoyed the privilege of sharing in this part of God's work here in PNG. However, my fall on the 4th of September, resulting in a broken leg and dislocated ankle bone had put quite an abrupt stop to much of my usual activities—and for a while to ALL of it! I'm happy to report, however, that presently I am able to move about quite well, using both legs, but still totally dependent on my crutches. They may be my companions yet for a couple more months, but at least it's getting easier all the time. Thanks so much to all of you who have prayed for us during these trying months.

Joy is now about to finish another school year in her ACE school here, and the Lord willing, she'll be continuing again in January of 1988 in a new setting somewhere in the USA. This is because we plan to be leaving PNG on the 20th of December—in just four weeks from now.

Therefore, with this update on the work here in Port Moresby, we also wish to add these few words of farewell to all the *MISSION MESSENGER* family, telling you how much we have appreciated being a part of the missionary family which you have been supporting with your prayers and gifts throughout the last 18 years that we have been here in PNG. While some of those years were rather difficult, we shall never regret having passed through them and experiencing all they have brought to us. God uses every detail of our lives to draw us closer to Himself, and we praise Him for helping us to benefit from our experiences—both good and bad. Nevertheless, we feel it is now God's time for us to step out from this area of ministry and wait for His further appointment in His own time and to the place of His choice.

Leaving both missionary and national friends behind in PNG will not be easy, but we trust God, Who is going before us and leading us step by step, to fill each gap with the grace and peace that comes from knowing that we are in His will. We ask your continued prayers for the work in Port Moresby, for our people whom we leave behind, for the national pastor—Moresby Tunge—who will be temporarily filling in until another missionary family is available, and for our family, as we are being renewed in body, soul, and spirit to take up our next appointment in God's vineyard. We shall still be *"laborers together"* for the Kingdom of God. Let us all be faithful until the end.

(The following comment was also written in the *Mission Messenger* by Gerald Bustin, *General Secretary of Evangelical Bible Mission* at the close of our ministry in Papua New Guinea—December, 1987.)

160

"It is with deep regret and sincere appreciation that we bid farewell to the Daniel Glick family. Brother and Sister Glick have served faithfully since 1969 when they first arrived on the field. They have left behind a beautiful track record of Christian Grace and Servant-hood. During their years of service, Brother Glick has served as Tambul Business Manager, Field Director, PNGBI Business Manager, Pastor of three town churches, and builder of over 50 churches and other buildings! Sister Glick has ably served as Teacher, Translator, Bookkeeper, Editor, and Mission Personnel Coordinator obtaining visas and work permits for the missionaries in Papua New Guinea.

Our sincere prayers and best wishes will go with the Glicks into the future God has for them."

As I re-read this commendation, my heart was humbled, yet overjoyed and filled with thanksgiving and praise to our *Lord and Savior, Jesus Christ.* All that has been done in and through us has been to bring praise and glory to *HIM*, and we have only been channels through which that praise and glory can be offered to Him. It is for this reason that I have written this book, that *GOD HIMSELF* might be praised and glorified through me as I recall all that *HE HAS DONE* in and through my life which from my youth had been *fully dedicated to Him*, cleaned by *the blood of Christ*, and *filled with His Holy Spirit.* I have not given details of some of the very difficult and troublesome times that I myself and Daniel and I together have gone through along the way, but that is because GOD has given us victory in every case, and those things need not be rehearsed any more! Praise the Lord!

Here are the words to a song that I would like to include, expressing my testimony quite well.

CHANNELS ONLY

How I praise You, precious Savior,
That Your love laid hold of me;
You have saved and cleansed and filled me,
That I might Your channel be.

Emptied, that You should fill me,
A clean vessel in Your hand;
With no power but as You give me,
Gloriously, with each command.

Jesus, fill now with Your Spirit
Hearts that full surrender know,
That the streams of living water
From their inner man may flow.

CHORUS
Channels only, blessed Master,
But with all Your wondrous power,
Flowing through us,
You can use us,
Every day and every hour.

———

What more can I say, dear reader. You have been very gracious to hear me out as I've told you some of the highlights of our lives in Papua New Guinea as missionaries. I could go on and on—especially if I could also show you the many photos we have taken, for each has a story of its own to tell. I have gleaned from them a few photos that will help you to picture some of the things, people, and places mentioned in the story.

(You will find more photos in the *Appendix* section of this book).

EPILOGUE

Our years of ministry with the *Evangelical Bible Mission* and the *PNG Bible Church* had come to a close, but the lives of our dear PNG missionary family and brothers and sisters of the PNG Bible Church are so intricately intertwined together in our hearts and minds that they will never be forgotten or removed from our memories—forever! We loved them then, and we still love them now. Although our follow-up contact with these dear people has not been frequent through the years that followed our departure from PNG (almost 24 years now), we have had some wonderful visits back to PNG since then. Also numerous individuals from PNG have come to visit USA or spend extended periods of time here attending school, and we have had some of them to visit us here in our home. Reunions with both missionaries and/or national PNG friends are always delightful and rejuvenating to our hearts and minds, creating anew a desire to spend some time in PNG with them again.

Truly it will be wonderful to re-connect with all of our beloved PNG brothers and sisters in the Lord once again in our forever home—*Heaven! Amen!*

In *PART III* of *"MY STORY"* you will read about the return visits we made to PNG—in 1994, 1998, 2005, and 2007, along with our ministries in Russia, Romania, Venezuela, Mexico, and in New Mexico among the Native American Navajos. Each ministry had its own set of challenges and rewards, and we praise God for His choice of fields for us to labor for His Kingdom and His glory.

APPENDIX

2007 STATISTICS
of the
PAPUA NEW GUINEA BIBLE CHURCH

Over 600 CHURCHES

Over 500 PASTORS

(25) CHURCH DISTRICTS
(15 or more churches in each *District*)

15 ACE SCHOOLS

PACIFIC BIBLE COLLEGE *(English)*
(Founded 1987)
TAMBUL BAIBEL SKUL *(Pidgin)*
(Founded 1972)
(Present Enrollment: 75 students)

(3) GOVERNMENT HIGH SCHOOLS
(on Mission Stations)

PAPUA NEW GUINEA BIBLE INSTITUTE:
(Grades 7-10) (1972-1987)
PNGBI changed to ACE SCHOOL
(for all ages) (1988 – Present)

NATIONAL LADIES' RETREAT

NATIONAL MEN'S RETREAT

NATIONAL YOUTH RETREAT

Photos taken at the 2007 Ladies' Retreat in Mt. Hagen, PNG
ABOVE: A crowd of 5000+ ladies gathered under and around the
huge tent for each of the sessions. BELOW: The ladies prepare to
march in groups to the Queen Elizabeth Park for a public rally. Each
group carries a banner representing its church district.

Nancy Rohrer | Esther Miller | Millard Downing | Naomi Downing | Ruth Glick | Helen Glick | Edward Miller

PENIEL HOLINESS CHRISTIAN DAY SCHOOL
HIGH SCHOOL DEPARTMENT
Staff and Students

1968-1969

Millard Downing, Principal

Susanna Hostetler | David Downing | Becky Helsel | Viola Miller

Graduates
of 1968
not pictured:
Henry Miller
Robert Miller
Mae Miller

Lane Glick | Wilma Glick | LaVina Glick | Christine Miller | Ray Miller | Clara Miller

Cathy Helsel | Rachel Yoder | Ida Miller | David Weaver | Mary Miller | Naomi Miller | Miriam Yoder

BELOW:
Kapi Kasi, his wife, son, and daughter—with whom we went to Lake Kutubu and began prison ministry in Mendi, Southern Highlands

Daniel is building a
driveway bridge
across the waterway.

BELOW:
The clear, fresh
waterway where the
school children
at Tambul
wash up for school

Joy and Michael Konjil

"Look, Michael, they want to take our picture."

Here, put your head up, and look straight into the camera.

Joy Regina Glick, age 17, (1987) at Port Moresby in her school uniform when attending the Gerehu Baptist Christian Academy

LEFT:
"They're ready!"
"Oh, the sun is too bright!"

This happy man is
returning from his garden,
laden with a bilum (string bag)
full of kaukau.
He is carrying his bush knife and axe,
which are used to clear bush areas
where new gardens are to be planted.
In his hand, he also has a folded umbrella
which is made of banana leaves.
His clothing is the typical garb
of a village man—including
his hand-woven hair cover,
his wide, bamboo belt (with tanget-leaves
tucked under the belt
to cover the back side of his body),
and his hand-woven,
multi-folded front body covering.
Hanging from his neck and on his
chest is a traditional *kina shell*—
which is one of the valuable,
economic treasures
of the people of
Papua New Guinea.

This is a typical village lady, carrying her child on her shoulders, and a bilum containing kaukau (sweet potatoes) from her garden. (Babies are also carried in a bilum in the same way that garden produced is carried.)

Her clothing consists only of a laplap, tied together at two corners and placed on top of her head, leaving the rest of the laplap hanging down over her back. She also has a traditional cluster of strings hanging from a band of strings around her waist, which extend all the way down to her ankles. These strings serve as a modesty covering for the front and back parts of her body.

LEFT:
A typical vine bridge we sometimes had to cross when going to Outstations

BELOW:
A typical bridge we often had to cross in our road travels

BELOW: A typical state of chaos when there was lots of rain and mud on the mountainous roads we had to travel

175

ABOVE: Inside the airport at Mt. Hagen. Note the colorful string bags. The lady on the right side of the picture has a baby in her bag.

BELOW: Another typical vine bridge crossing a swift-flowing river

Pastor Kalepo with his family at his house in Mendi where we lived while he was on leave

RIGHT:
An outstation church near Mendi—One of the many Daniel built

Primary School children who were in my Religious Instruction Class at Mendi

LEFT:
Under our house at Mt. Hagen from where our car was stolen.

RIGHT:
Daniel built the stone wall and concrete floor for our worship area under the house.

LEFT:
It's time for our worship service. (The slatted roof is covered with plastic and lets in the light.)

Our Subaru, as we found it after being stolen from under our house in Gerehu

The church, school, & toilet block Daniel built in the city of Lae, Morobe Province

A special treat for Joy, but Daddy is having fun, too!

Celebrating a Birthday after a Bible Study inside our house at Gerehu

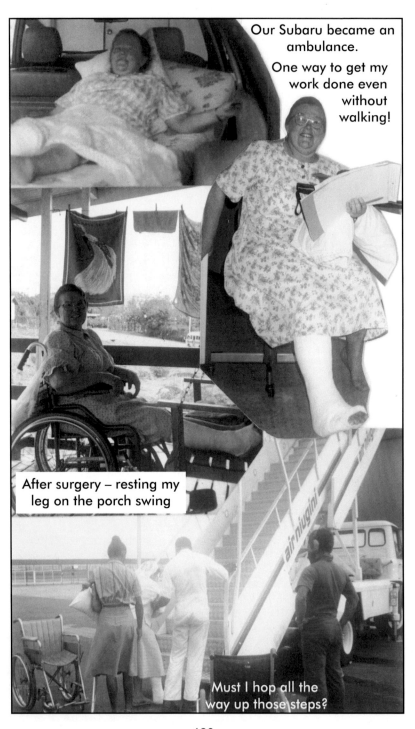

Our Subaru became an ambulance.

One way to get my work done even without walking!

After surgery – resting my leg on the porch swing

Must I hop all the way up those steps?

Ladies preparing food for a "mumu"—which is a way to cook food in a hole dug in the ground. The hole is first lined with large green leaves (such as banana leaves.) Then the food—meat, and a variety of vegetables and greens are put in the hole, mixed with HOT rocks and covered with more green leaves. Last, the hole is covered with ground to seal the heat inside and steam-cook the food for several hours. When the hole is opened and the food is carefully removed, it is a tasty meal for any feast or special occasion!
Ummm, delicious!

Air view of the *Pabarabuk Station* with the airstrip down the center—the location of the *Papua New Guinea Bible Institute where we lived from 1974-1980*

1. Rose's House (The BLACK House)
2. Pelfrey's House
3. Piggery
4. Joinery Shop & Workers' Houses
5. Dining Room, Kitchen, & Classroom
6. Mrs. Lorknor's House
7. Glick's House (Daniel built)
8. Sewing room, Library, Print Shop
9. PNGBI Classrooms
10. Boys' Dormitorie
11. New Prayer Chapel & Classrooms

12 Two Single Teacher's Houses
13. Bible Center Classroom
14. Antrim's House
15. Girls' Dormitory
16. Pastor Philip's House
17. Taylor's House
18. Wehrman's House
19. Fruit/ and Tool House
20. Local Church
22. Sib-Health Center
23. Mechanic Shop & Classroom

MY STORY

Will be continued

in a

Third Volume

Part 3
(1988-2012)

(as funds are available)

This volume will include stories of ministries in
Russia and Romania
As well as short-term projects in Venezuela,
And the Brethren-in-Christ Mission
Among the Navajo of New Mexico